BUYING A
COUNTRY HOUSE

A REGIONAL GUIDE TO VALUE

COUNTRY LIFE

BUYING A
COUNTRY HOUSE

A REGIONAL GUIDE TO VALUE
IN ASSOCIATION WITH
KNIGHT FRANK & RUTLEY

PUBLISHED BY
COUNTRY LIFE

IN ASSOCIATION WITH
Knight Frank
& Rutley

Designed by Slade Hamilton Fenech Ltd,
and edited by Michael Wright.

Printed by Clifford Frost Ltd, Lyon Road,
Windsor Avenue, Wimbledon, London
SW19 2SE.

WE LOOK AFTER OUR CLIENTS' MONEY AS IF IT WERE OUR OWN.

After all, we are simply continuing a great tradition. Henderson Administration was originally established for the sole purpose of managing the financial affairs of the Henderson family. Their need for a confidential, personal service, with investment flair, shaped the standards by which we have grown.

Today, Henderson remains an independent company. True, we have diversified into investment trusts, unit trusts and pension funds, but managing the investment portfolios of prosperous private individuals is still as fundamental to our business as ever.

For this reason, an exclusive feature of the Henderson approach is the Asset Manager, assigned to each private client and personally accountable for the highest level of professional attention.

The Henderson service is available to those with £150,000 or more to invest. For full details please telephone or write to Alistair Mackechnie or David Browne at Henderson Financial Management Limited, 26 Finsbury Square, London, EC2. Telephone: 01-638 5757.

OUR FIRST CLIENT.
ALEXANDER HENDERSON 1850-1934
FIRST LORD FARINGDON.

HENDERSON FINANCIAL MANAGEMENT

HENDERSON ADMINISTRATION GROUP plc

BUYING A
COUNTRY HOUSE

A REGIONAL GUIDE TO VALUE

CONTENTS

PUBLISHED BY

COUNTRY LIFE

IN ASSOCIATION WITH

Knight Frank
& Rutley

KF+R

4

FOREWORD

Ownership of a country house is a necessity for some people, a symbol of success to others; sometimes an unrealisable dream. To many it is simply home. Any decision about where and what to buy is based on a complex mixture of emotive and objective issues. This book is intended to provide would-be buyers with some researched information on objective issues: past investment performance, value for money, environment, facilities and communications.

Most investors in equities or fixed interest securities base their investment decisions on advice given to them by experts, who have available to them detailed research. Many forms of analysis are used by fund managers who invest in commercial property, all of whom are either experts on the subject themselves or seek expert advice.

In spite of the fact that, to most of us, our house represents the single most important investment we have, few people seek professional advice when buying, and very little researched information is readily available on the subject. Many of the Building Societies publish statistics on house-price movements, both nationally and regionally, but these mainly concern new houses, estate houses or those in urban areas where some common denominator is evident. No such common denominator exists in the case of country houses, where the price of a six-bedroom Queen Anne house will differ greatly from that of an Edwardian house of the same size in a similar location. No two are the same.

Our research department has drawn information from a very large selection of country house sales undertaken by us over the last five years and has distilled this into a form of analysis which we believe will provide the reader with a fair assessment of the movement in country house prices, region by region, over the period. In each case this is shown as a comparison against a national indicator and the information

has been drawn together to illustrate relative investment performance.

Any given sum of money will buy significantly more in one area of the country than it will in another and we have included some guidance on where to seek 'value for money'. This inevitably means those regions which for one reason or another have been or are less in demand. The most common factor in this respect is the communication between respective locations and London, other major conurbations and international airports. With ever-increasing pressures placed upon the executive workforce, the question of how easy it is to get to work, whether by aeroplane, train or car, is of major importance, and we have devoted a section to this subject.

Knight Frank and Rutley has had a long and close relationship with COUNTRY LIFE. Walton and Lee, who merged with Knight Frank and Rutley in 1911 had the front page advertisement in COUNTRY LIFE when the magazine was first published in 1897, and this contract has been renewed ever since. KFR folklore has it that this was the very thing that caused Sir Howard Frank, a great entreprenurial marketing man, to seek the merger. Although the firm is now a world-wide group of 43 offices dealing with all types of property, its name is synonymous with the sale of country houses, farms and estates in the British Isles. The tens of thousands of such properties which we have sold are all documented in our records. These include the most complete collection of COUNTRY LIFE issues in existence, due to the fact that many of the magazine's own records were destroyed in the war. Hence who more natural for us to turn to in seeking a publisher than COUNTRY LIFE. They have enriched our research with descriptions of the regions covered and a number of interesting articles by their regular contributors.

Country houses come in all types and sizes from cottages to castles. Although we cover much of the country, there are areas for which we have an insufficient cross-section of evidence from our own records upon which to base our research. We therefore acknowledge and thank a number of locally based firms of estate agents, with whom we have worked over the years, who have assisted us.

We intend to continue our analysis and with the help of COUNTRY LIFE make this an annual publication, in the hope that prospective buyers of country houses will be helped in their selection of locations.

BILL YATES
Head, Residential Division, Knight Frank and Rutley.

COUNTY INDEX

SOUTH EAST

1 ESSEX
2 HERTFORDSHIRE
3 BUCKINGHAMSHIRE
4 OXFORDSHIRE
5 BERKSHIRE
6 SURREY
7 KENT

SOUTH

8 SUSSEX
9 HAMPSHIRE

WEST

10 GLOUCESTERSHIRE
11 AVON
12 HEREFORD & WORCESTER
13 WILTSHIRE

SOUTH WEST

14 SOMERSET
15 DORSET
16 DEVON
17 CORNWALL

EAST ANGLIA

18 CAMBRIDGESHIRE
19 SUFFOLK
20 NORFOLK

EAST MIDLANDS

21 BEDFORDSHIRE
22 NORTHAMPTONSHIRE
23 LINCOLNSHIRE
24 DERBYSHIRE
25 NOTTINGHAMSHIRE
26 LEICESTERSHIRE

WEST MIDLANDS

27 WARWICKSHIRE
28 SHROPSHIRE
29 CHESHIRE
30 STAFFORDSHIRE

NORTH

31 YORKSHIRE
32 NORTHUMBERLAND
33 HUMBERSIDE
34 DURHAM
35 CUMBRIA
36 LANCASHIRE

SCOTLAND

37 LOWLANDS & HIGHLANDS

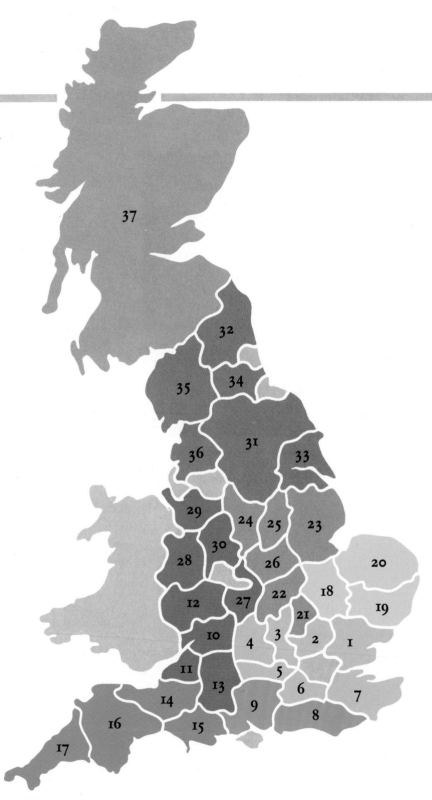

PUBLISHED BY **COUNTRY LIFE** IN ASSOCIATION WITH

Knight Frank & Rutley

HOW TO USE
BUYING A
COUNTRY HOUSE

Although many statistics are regularly published on the movement of house prices both nationally and regionally, this information only covers new property, and primarily only that in urban areas. COUNTRY LIFE magazine and Knight Frank and Rutley have accordingly sought to provide similar information for country houses, and based on a selection of the numerous sales undertaken by Knight Frank and Rutley over the past five years, their research department has analysed the changes in the prices paid for these fine country houses region by region, and compared this with a national indicator to illustrate relative investment performance of different areas of the country.

The map on the opposite page shows how the country has been divided up for the purposes of this book and the individual counties gathered under regional headings, which have been colour-coded throughout BUYING A COUNTRY HOUSE. Each county has been treated in a similar fashion: a map locates the area under discussion, and a picture in words and photographs is given of the main geographical features of the county, its cities and principal market towns, the opportunities that exist for recreation, and the fine houses and gardens in the area, some in the hands of the National Trust and other privately owned. This portrait of each county is also illustrated by photographs of fine country houses considered to be typical of the area. A final section for each county deals with the important subject of communications with London, by road, rail and, where appropriate, by air. In every case where commuting is possible, the time of the train that will enable you to reach London at approximately 8.30 a.m. is also given.

Pages 94, 96 and 98 at the conclusion of the regional chapters offer a summary of the statistical information and descriptive material under the title 'Value at a Glance'. It is clear that distance from London is an important factor in the variations that there have been in country house prices during the past few years, but it is interesting nonetheless that conurbations such as Birmingham and Manchester have exerted their own attractions. Greater ease of communications has enabled some parts of the country to show higher levels of growth than others not so well favoured. Perhaps the most difficult question uppermost in the minds of all considering the purchase of a country house is to determine how much of the value of a house or estate can strictly be regarded as an investment. This is discussed in 'Value at a Glance', but further assistance on this subject and on the vexed question of liability for tax is given in Adrian Baird's introductory article on page 16.

Throughout the book the same colour coding has been used on all the maps, and a key to the symbols used for National Parks, Areas of Outstanding Natural Beauty, rivers, roads and railway lines and so on is shown on this page.

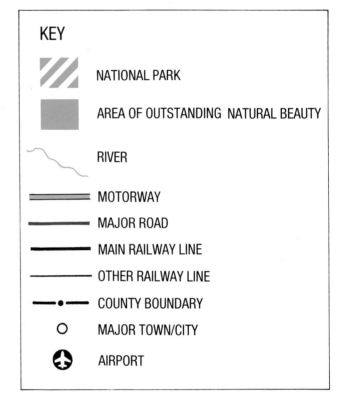

KEY

NATIONAL PARK

AREA OF OUTSTANDING NATURAL BEAUTY

RIVER

MOTORWAY

MAJOR ROAD

MAIN RAILWAY LINE

OTHER RAILWAY LINE

COUNTY BOUNDARY

MAJOR TOWN/CITY

AIRPORT

CHANGING ATTITUDES TO COUNTRY

People have been buying COUNTRY LIFE for 90 years to enjoy their dream of country living. Nowhere in the magazine is that dream more substantial than in the opening pages of advertisements for country houses. These have been dominated for years by one firm, Knight Frank & Rutley, who have handled the sale or purchase of some of the most historic houses in Britain, such as Sir Winston Churchill's Chartwell, Evelyn Waugh's Combe Florey, Viscount Massereene's Chilham Castle and David Astor's Compton Beauchamp.

For many readers, the pleasure is the vicarious one of imagining that one owns (or could afford to buy) some of the beautiful houses so temptingly displayed. Nor is this covetousness restricted to those of slender means. A man whose ancestors have inhabited a draughty castle for centuries may well envy one who lives in a warm, thatched cottage; but where would he hang the family portraits? Someone who can afford £1 million for a house may envy another who can pay £10 million for one.

The trouble with country houses, as with motor cars, is that they are all things to all men, and every house is a compromise. Just as one needs a stable of six cars to accommodate all one's various motoring needs, so one needs a variety of houses to meet the needs of a family at different times and (because houses are not mobile) places.

Some people are fortunate enough to have more than one property, but the ownership of second homes in Britain is astonishingly low — fewer than two per cent of households.

Perhaps this is not surprising in a Puritan country that taxes everything beyond one's principal place of residence (and only allows an acre of garden with it, or such larger area that is deemed to be appropriate to the character and quality of the house).

So the country house is a compromise for most people. Should it be one's principal place of residence, from which one commutes to town? Or should it be the bolthole to which one escapes at weekends or whenever the metropolitan pressures become too great? If so, how far away should it be?

As Britain's countryside has changed, so have attitudes to country houses. One may marvel at how the King's courtiers in medieval England could travel to the Palace of Whitehall from the farthest points in the kingdom, but it is the accessibility of the countryside today that puts the greatest premium on the price of houses. Not for nothing are the areas nearest to London known as the Home Counties.

Apart from accessibility, however, what matters most is the quality of the countryside. So the Cotswolds, the Lake District, the Peak District and the Yorkshire Dales have a magic that has nothing to do with ease of access. Indeed, their fragile beauty is threatened by their very popularity, and those who live in such beautiful surroundings do not want to make it possible for others to destroy what they professedly come to admire.

So what is it that people are seeking when they set out to buy a house in the country? The open spaces, the trees, the birds and the flowers go without saying. Or do they? Many

HOUSES *By* MICHAEL HANSON

people want to live in the country without being of the country, so they look for a house in a country town or village, where their neighbours are as close as they would be in London, Birmingham or Manchester, but with the advantage of having the real countryside almost on their doorstep.

Others want that real countryside for themselves. They want the distance from their neighbours, the silence of solitude, the blackness of night without streetlamps, the smell of the fertiliser and the roar of the crows. Above all, they want space, in or around their house. The house itself may not be big (it may even be a cottage), but it may have a garden larger than one could afford in town, or views longer than the houses in between allow in the city.

They may want to ride to hounds, or simply to have a paddock for a pony. They may want to fish or shoot, or simply to commune with nature. They may want outbuildings in which to have room to pursue their arts or crafts, or to indulge their hobbies or house their collections. They may want land for growing flowers, or breeding fish or fowl.

In the pages that follow, all country life is here. From the manor house to the cottage, from the farmhouse to the former rectory, from the mill house to the converted barn. Overcrowded as it is, Britain is still a country dotted with settlements, and it is the country life that many people yearn for as they pursue their personal fortunes in the cities.

The 900th anniversary of Domesday last year reminded us how remarkably little Britain has changed. The nucleus of the country town or village is still the parish church, with its parsonage, the manor house, an inn, the farms and cottages, and perhaps even a watermill or windmill. What has changed is the uses of some of those buildings.

The manor house may still be occupied by a descendant of its original builder, but that is increasingly rare. At best, it may still be in private occupation, or preserved by the National Trust, but more probably it has been converted into flats, a school, a hotel or even offices. At worst, it may be standing empty, awaiting a saviour, or it may be in ruins. One of the more encouraging manifestations of the new prosperity of Britain in recent years is that successful entrepreneurs are showing a desire to use their wealth to buy and restore some of our more historic houses.

It is not only the country mansion or manor house that may be too large for its traditional use. The Georgian or Victorian rectory next to the church is now unlikely to be occupied by the parson, for more than 2,000 have been sold by the Church in the past decade, and the proceeds used to build smaller modern houses for the clergy. Old rectories are a common feature of the country property market, offering spacious accommodation for those who can afford it.

Watermills and mill houses are seldom a setting for grinding corn or producing power today, but they are popular

The country house symbolises all that is best in country living: quality and dignity, space and seclusion. *(Far left)* **Tile-hanging and mellowed brickwork in Surrey.** *(Below)* **A substantial stone house in Leicestershire.**

with those who want to be near the water. It should be noted that they do not always come with the right to fish the waters that flow past them, for fishing rights (and shooting rights) are treated as a separate commodity in the countryside.

Farmhouses are often occupied today by those whose knowledge of farming is limited to listening to *The Archers,* just as the inside of many charming country cottages have not been seen by a swineherd or dairymaid this century. Indeed, the dream rather than the reality of country life is often seen at its best in farmhouses that have no land, and cottages whose pretensions of modesty do not extend to their prices.

For price rather than position is the biggest barrier to many who would like to live in the country (or the sanitised version of it that passes for countryside in much of the Home Counties). Cottages at £200,000 or more seem to be a contradiction in terms, but that is the price of proximity to the M3 or M4.

Those to whom the reality is more important than the dream are happy to forgo the convenience of rapid road or rail access for a property that they can afford. That is why properties are cheaper in Kent and Essex than in Surrey or Sussex, better value for money in Dorset and Wiltshire than in Hampshire or Gloucestershire, and easier to afford in Bedfordshire and Lincolnshire than in Berkshire or

Buckinghamshire. The same is true in the Midlands, where Derbyshire, Staffordshire and Herefordshire come cheaper than Warwickshire or Worcestershire (which only masquerades at being in the same county as Hereford).

In the North, it is a measure of the two faces of Britain that one can buy a country house *and* enough land to support it for less than the price of a semi-detached house in a suburb of London. A palace in the Palatines of Cheshire or Lancashire is the price of a pseudo-Tudor stockbroker's house in Pangbourne.

More than anything else, the 'Big Bang' in the City of London has altered people's attitudes to country houses. For one thing, it has produced overnight a generation of young people who can afford to buy the houses that their elders have been struggling to keep up for years. For another, it has magnified the importance of accessibility to London, resulting in the present distortion of property prices in the South-east. The stockbroker who now has to be in front of his SEAQ computer at 7 a.m. does not want to live too far away from London.

Britain is a tiny island, yet it encompasses a greater variety of property than one can find in most other countries. Here in the pages of this new property guide is an overview of the range of properties and the reasons why they continue to be so sought after by a population that, according to all the statistics, lives and works in the towns and cities. Perhaps, with the spread of telecommunication systems that allow people to work from home, this guide is as much a glimpse of tomorrow's world as a romantic ideal of a rural past.

Thatch and brick in Wiltshire: cottages are sought more for their romantic appeal than the harsh reality of rural life that they used to represent.

THE LEGACY OF THE COUNTRY HOUSE

The long, unmade-up drive . . . the dogs running round the car as you arrive . . . the garden flowers in the hall . . . the log fires in the grate . . . the beguiling books by the bedside . . . perhaps even the distinctive smell of wet leather in the gun room: these images are part of the irresistible appeal of the English country house. In no other country in the world has such a continuous effort been made to elevate leisure, or the appearance of it, to a finely judged art. Taken together with the landscape, gardening, architecture and collecting that go to make up a country house, it can be called Britain's greatest contribution to civilization.

According to the German observer, Hermann Muthesius, who wrote a monumental work on contemporary English houses at the turn of the century, history has been slowly working towards the perfection of the English house, and the way of life it expresses, for centuries. By 1900, he believed, the house had reached a point of refinement that was unequalled in Europe.

In some ways this typically Germanic approach seems gravely outdated today. One of the things that he particularly admired in the English house was the multiplicity of rooms, which he regarded as highly functional since it gave each task its allotted space. Two World Wars and comparative economic decline have made boot rooms and brushing rooms seem somewhat less practical. In the circumstances it is less surprising that so much has changed than that such an incredible amount of what Muthesius would have known still survives. For although many of the very large houses have gone, life still flourishes in innumerable medium-sized houses. Gardening has become a national passion. There is more interest in the countryside and wildlife than ever before. The country look, epitomised by Laura Ashley and Ralph Lauren, is high fashion. Country houses arouse popular interest as never before.

The country house and its surroundings are a framework to a way of life; and just as the manner in which people choose to live their lives is subject to infinite variety, so too, happily, are English country houses. There are three main variables. One, of course, is age and its bedfellow, architectural style. Your ideal might be a crinkum-crankum timbered farmhouse, with leaded lights, wobbly-looking beams and a roof covered in moss. The next man or woman may yearn after a sober Georgian box, with beautifully laid brickwork and that comfortable feeling of solidity, more than romance. Someone else, putting a tape of Wagner into the car cassette player, may head for Victorian neo-Gothic.

The other two variables are more subtle, and partake of the land itself. In which part of the country is your house to be found? Even within the immediate radius of London there are wonderful variations of landscape. Driving through the lanes of Surrey — a county bounteously supplied with large houses — you might hardly see evidence of human life at all, beyond, perhaps, a smoking chimneypot peeping above the pines. Surrey, sometimes sneered at by those who dwell in

(Below) **A handsome squire's house of about 1700 in Norfolk.** *(Right)* **Behind the Kentish 17th-century brickwork, lies a half-timbered yeoman's house.**

By **CLIVE ASLET**

more spacious country, is really one of the highest achievements of British culture, for a hundred years of intense development has not destroyed its beauty. Hidden among hills and woods, Surrey's houses remain a secret, both from passers by and from each other. Only a little further south and you are on the Sussex Downs: real country, with sweeping views. It was a bleak region before the Victorian period, and the sensible farmers who won their living from this chalky land liked to shelter from the wind. Their houses snuggled down in the valleys, pulling a blanket of trees around their ears.

Looking to the east is Kent. You might think of Kent as a county of round hills and small fields, of apple trees and rows of hops. Yet it also has what, in its way, is some of the most spectacular coastline in Britain, the wide expanse of Romney Marsh always conjuring up the image of arriving Roman legionaries.

Moving up the coast you come to Essex and Suffolk. How fortunate they have been in the A12, still the most awkward route out of London! This, and a traditionally bad train service, has allowed them to slip into the late 20th century in a remarkable degree of preservation. One fears for them now that the Chelmsford by-pass is open and the line to Liverpool Street has been electrified. This is flat, open country, rather too open in parts, thanks to intensive grain farming. It is also Constable country. Cambridgeshire makes no claim to conventional beauty, but Cambridge itself is so pleasing that one cannot be surprised that an ever-increasing number of people want to live there. It takes a tough kind of

spirit to live in the Fens, with its huge sky and blood-orange sunsets and memories of Dorothy L. Sayer's *The Nine Taylors*. Altogether cosier is the hilly Oxfordshire landscape which turns into the Cotswolds as you follow it west. It is incredible to think that the Cotswolds were once regarded as gaunt and unappealing: they seem the very antithesis today.

This circular sweep around London ends in Berkshire, where there is yet another kind of landscape in the wide open horse-racing country of the Berkshire Downs. And all this wide choice lies within a couple of hours, at most, of the capital. Venture a little beyond the usual week-ending distance and you find the heaths of Dorset and the orchards of Herefordshire; beyond them the flower-laden lanes of Cornwall and the ancient mountains of Wales. If you go North; oh dear! Space does not permit me to expand further.

The third variable depends on the materials of the region. After 1840 or so this ceased to be of much importance: the railways meant that large quantities of bricks and tiles and slates could be moved round the country at comparatively little cost, which destroyed the old local feeling of architecture. This was revived by a few earnest souls at the turn of the century, but by and large things have not been the same since. In the days when transport was not easily available, however, most people had to be content with what they could find near at hand. In some counties there is admirable building stone. A band of limestone sweeps upwards in a boomerang-shape from the Dorset coast to the Wash. Here, around Bath, Oxford, Stamford, Lincoln, you will find stone houses with silver grey or buff-coloured walls

and sometimes even mossy stone roofs. The stone, or some of it, lends itself to decorative work such as balusters, pilasters and finials. Sandstone of a red hue was readily available in the Midlands. There is good building stone all over Scotland.

Other areas, such as Cheshire, East Anglia and much of the south-east of England, are not so blessed. Flints, dug up from chalky ground and then split or knapped to give a flat, shiny surface, were one possibility. Though less than ideal they are used more in England than in any other country in the world. In the medieval period the obvious alternative to stone was wood and an elaborate technology developed for constructing the timber frame of a dwelling. Sometimes one floor was jettied out over another as a piece of bravado, and the exposed timbers were carved for ornament. But it can be a tricky business identifying what really does date from the 15th or 16th centuries in a house of this kind, for often it will have gone through many changes in the course of its long life — going out of fashion in the 18th century and almost certainly being divided up internally, before being rescued, and no doubt enlarged and embellished, in the 1920s.

More timber-frame buildings survive than one might at first realise, because, whether for ornament or weatherproofing, the frame was often concealed. This applies particularly to houses of more modest status. In East Anglia, the technique of decorative plasterwork known as pargeting was, and is, a speciality. Tile-hanging — placing overlapping tiles vertically on walls as well as roof — is particularly seen in Kent and Sussex. Many timber houses came to be simply encased in brick.

Brick is an exceedingly old material, but until the 17th century it was laborious to make and therefore a luxury. Chimneys were of necessity made of brick, and such was the bricklayer's art that they could be wrought into fantastic shapes. But it took a very rich man indeed to build a house completely of brick. In the late 17th and 18th centuries it became less costly and swung into fashion with a vengeance. But still, partly for reasons of transport, production was not centralised, and there are glorious variations in the old bricks to be found throughout Britain. For the result depended not only on the available clay but on the skill of the itinerant brickmaker who baked it. Red, yellow, buff and brown: these are the commonest colours. In Suffolk so-called white bricks give a characteristically austere look to many houses.

In the Victorian period, regional individuality was replaced by the individuality of the architect's imagination. The materials of a Victorian house are more predictable, but sometimes the architecture is less so. But even the wildest Gothic Revival horror can be made into an appealing country house, because architecture is, after all, only part of the experience. Trees, lawns, gardens, country air — not to mention open fires, old furniture, a well-stocked drinks cupboard and a large dining table — these are some of the things that are part of a country house. Achieving the right note of inevitability, which yet has your own personality in it too, is a challenge equal to that of the old builders.

Dreamy Edwardian romanticism, in Sussex.

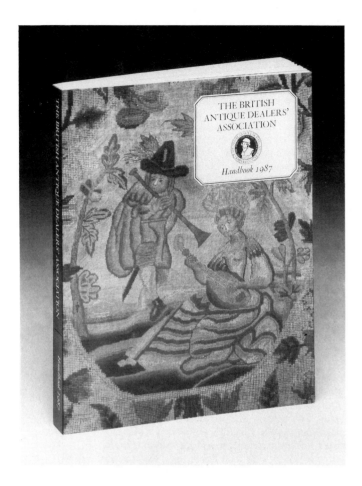

THE IDEAL PRESENT

SECOND EDITION

Illustrated in colour throughout

194 pages

Handbook 1987

A select and informative guide to some of the foremost antique dealers in Britain, designed to help those wishing to buy or sell fine antiques and works of art in the UK.

This Handbook is the British Antique Dealers' Association guide to its distinguished membership giving concise and up-to-date particulars about their shops and the antiques in which they specialise, together with regional maps showing their locations. Beautifully illustrated throughout, the Handbook contains a collection of unusual articles by leading experts, as well as useful information on import and export regulations, and a diary of major UK antiques fairs for 1987.

This is an important reference book for all discriminating buyers of antiques, and a handsome addition to the bookshelf or coffee table.

Available from your bookseller price £7.50 or direct from the BADA using the coupon below.

The British Antique Dealers' Association
20 Rutland Gate
London SW7 1BD
Telephone: 01-589 4128

AVOIDING TAXATION'S BURDEN

Avoiding the unnecessary payment of taxes should be everyone's maxim, but landowners often are very reluctant to adopt it. I have often wondered why this should be. Perhaps it is feared that the awful complexity of tax planning for an estate or country house could ruin what has been acquired for enjoyment. But taxes, like the other thing which can never be avoided, creep up on a landowner by stealth. This article attempts to outline the main points to consider and to urge the would-be owner of a fine country property to seek out professional guidance before completing the purchase.

The first thing to consider will often be the land surrounding the house. In most cases this will consist of a tract of pastoral beauty which can broadly be described as agricultural land. If that land is already occupied by a secured agricultural tenant, then the management of the land will not be a major problem. However, if the land is vacant ('in-hand') then the question of management and occupation should be one of the first matters to resolve. Reliefs from various taxes (especially capital taxes) are more freely available where the owner occupies the land.

But not everyone has the time or desire to run the estate. There are three broad options here. Firstly, to retain the land in-hand and manage the estate as an owner-occupier. Secondly, the land can be rented either under a secured tenancy or under a short-term licence. Thirdly, the possibility of a 'share-farming' arrangement should be considered.

The Owner-occupier
The owner-occupier has several advantages over the landlord. For income tax purposes, the income arising from the estate should be classed as earned income from a trade. Consequently, losses (subject to certain restrictions) can be set against other income. For Capital Gains Tax, the possibility of deferring or exempting gains arising on a future sale could be worth considerable sums of money. In respect of Inheritance Tax, owner-occupied land should qualify for a 50 per cent reduction in value after two years' ownership.

In general, the simpler the structure of ownership the easier it will be to obtain these benefits. Sole proprietorship or a partnership of joint owners should cause few problems. Where, however, the business is run by a company, far more conditions usually have to be met for these tax benefits to accrue.

Also rather nasty taxable benefits can arise especially where the company is also the owner of the property. Nevertheless, companies do provide several advantages, for instance, relatively low rates of corporation tax or self-administered pension schemes. Professional advice is essential to arrive at the most beneficial decision.

Landlords
Although the landlord may not have the same tax advantages as the owner-occupier, there may be very good non-fiscal reasons why this option is chosen or forced upon the owner. Generally the rental income will be regarded as unearned (at present not more heavily taxed, but what of the future?). The main exception will be where the land is let out on a short-term grazing licence. Provided such a licence is properly

A substantial brick house in Oxfordshire with decorative tile-hanging.

A Cheshire property backed by amenity woodland.

By **ADRIAN BAIRD**

A charming Surrey estate of the Regency period.

drawn it can still be possible for the owner to be regarded as a farmer and not a landlord, by selling a 'crop', that is the grass itself.

It may be that the owner will want to let the land to a trusted relative who is able to manage the land. If so, it is invariably correct to make sure that the rent set is fully commercial, and independent valuations should be sought. However, the main tax disadvantages to the landlord are to be found in the capital taxes. The landlord will suffer Capital Gains Tax on a future sale and the Inheritance Tax relief is limited to 30 per cent and is only available after seven years ownership. Letting land to a company controlled by the owner or to a partnership can be a way around the problem, but there are many pitfalls for the unwary.

The Share Farmer
Share farming is an innovative alternative to both owner-occupation and letting land. Its practice is firmly established in Australasia and in America. Broadly, the landowner and another, the operator, enter into an agreement which ensures that both are separately carrying on a business and occupying the land. This means that the owner should retain all the fiscal advantages available to the owner-occupier and yet be free from most of the day-to-day management problems, which

are carried out by the operator. It is most important that the share-farming agreement is what it purports to be otherwise a tenancy may be unwittingly created. For this reason it is best to seek guidance from a specialist in this area.

Woodlands
The tax position of woodlands will depend to a great extent on whether the woodlands are commercial and managed as such, or are merely amenity woodlands for the rest of the land. Most people know that commercial woodlands are favourably taxed at present, and the taxpayer has a real choice as to the basis on which he is taxed.

Here much will depend on the age of the woodlands and the value of being able to set losses against other income. It is usually important for capital tax purposes that the accounts of the woodland are separated from the rest of the estate. Amenity woodlands, on the other hand, are broadly taxed in the same way as the surrounding land.

Sporting Rights
It may be that the new owner is fortunate to acquire sporting rights over the land. If the estate has been purchased to use those rights, many annoying tax problems can arise. For example, with shooting it may be that the owner wishes to

A large stone-built Yorkshire house in its own land.

A fine stone house in Dorset set in mature gardens.

organise shoots for his friends and their families. The way the shoots are organised needs careful consideration otherwise the owner may face an unexpected bill for VAT.

Shoots need beaters and the PAYE treatment of wages paid to beaters can cause many headaches. Again, the professional adviser should be able to guide the owner through the numerous revenue statements and practices on this subject. One topical warning: HM Customs and Excise is presently trying to levy VAT on the purchase of land with sporting rights attached. The outcome of this case is not at present known. Prudent purchasers would be well advised to try to obtain more details about it, and about the judgement.

The Great House

The house is likely to be a major part of the purchase price and may well be the main reason for the purchase of the estate. Most people know that a principal private residence is exempt from Capital Gain Tax. However, where two or more residences are owned the owner has a right to decide to which this valuable tax exemption is to be applied. This need not be the one which he regards as home. It should be noted that, if the owner does not exercise this right to choose within two years of purchase, then the choice moves to the Inland Revenue.

Further, the exemption only applies to the residence and up to one acre of land *unless* the owner can demonstrate that a larger area of land is 'reasonably required' for the enjoyment of the residence. The use to which the curtilage of the house is put could be very important here. It is always wise to retain the sales brochure and take some pictures of the house and surrounding land on purchase, as it could be useful evidence in future.

Owner-occupiers who manage the surrounding land as a business may be able to obtain relief for a proportion of household expenses. Furthermore, capital improvements may qualify for agricultural buildings allowance, although this is by no means as valuable as it once was. For Inheritance Tax purposes the agricultural value of the house may also qualify for relief.

Where the house or surrounding land is listed, it may be possible to obtain capital tax reliefs for Heritage Property. These tax reliefs are not only available on the property itself but also apply to maintenance funds set up for the property. Unfortunately these tax reliefs are obtained by entering into certain conditions, and the penalties for breaking them are severe. There is a very useful booklet published on this subject entitled *Capital Taxation and the National Heritage* (priced £5.20, available from the Inland Revenue, Somerset House, London).

Wills and the Estate

The purchase of a country estate is also an ideal time to consider present wills. Often it will be important to consider alterations to dispositions to make sure that Inheritance Tax is kept to a minimum.

However, it should be remembered that in the tax world death is not final. The beneficiaries have two years in which to alter dispositions for capital tax purposes. This can allow the various reliefs and exemptions to be re-appraised on death to maximum advantage. Much more flexibility is available, however, where estates are equalised so neither spouse owns the entire property. This suggests that the ownership should be carefully considered. The question should be asked, for instance, whether the estate should be bought in joint names.

The Moral: Act on Good Advice

When I leave the telephones and word processors of London behind every month to give advice to landowners in the regions, the peace is invariably shattered by someone who realises his estate is soon to be decimated (or worse) by taxes. There is little I can do to help where too little tax planning has been done. The moral must be to act early on good advice and with a bit of luck you will not only enjoy what you have bought but also preserve it for the future.

THE COTSWOLD ANTIQUE DEALERS' ASSOCIATION

A wealth of Antiques in the heart of England

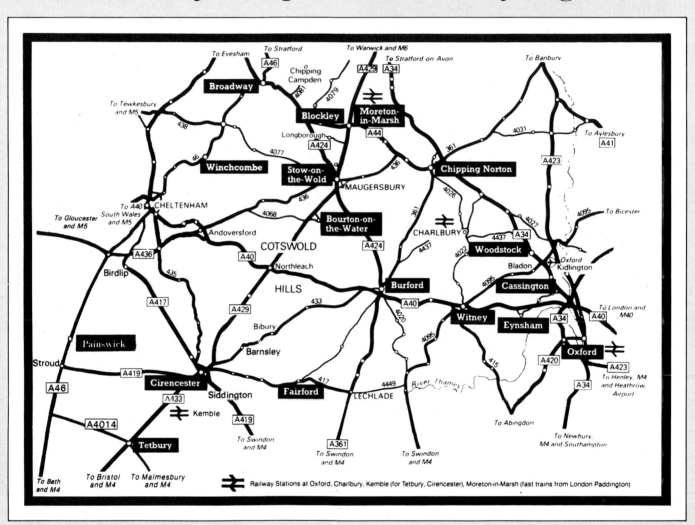

Railway Stations at Oxford, Charlbury, Kemble (for Tetbury, Cirencester), Moreton-in-Marsh (fast trains from London Paddington)

The C.A.D.A. represents a group of Antique Dealers situated in the heart of England. Our aims are to promote and encourage trade in the Cotswold area and to assist all visiting dealers and collectors in locating antiques and works of art.

Our members will give advice on where to stay in the area, assistance with packing, shipping, insurance and exchange of foreign currencies.

The Cotswolds are within easy reach of London (1½ hours by road or rail) and several major airports.

Our association welcomes home and overseas buyers with the certain knowledge that there are at least 50 dealers with a good and varied stock, a reputation for fair trading and an annual turnover in excess of £11,000,000.

Fine antiques and works of art at provincial prices in England's lovely and historic countryside.

For free colour brochure and members' directory, please contact:

The Secretary, C.A.D.A., High Street, Blockley, nr. Moreton-in-Marsh, Glos. Tel: 0386 700280

ESSEX

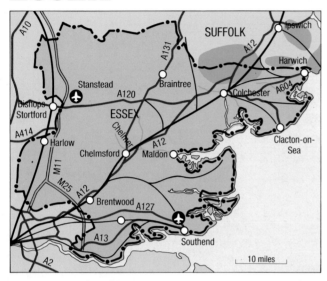

GEOGRAPHY

To anyone emerging into Essex from the northern end of the Dartford tunnel on M25, the impression of Essex is of an industrialised county. In reality it is not, outside the highly urbanised and partly industrialised London periphery. Dagenham, for example, is in London, not in Essex. The landscape is gently undulating, with no sizeable hills. In common with other parts of East Anglia, farming, though once mixed, is now largely arable. In the north west of the county the land rises to about 350 ft., enhancing the river valleys, but in the east and south the sea predominates causing erosion that Essex has had to fight for generations. Even today, the foreshore in parts of the county is sinking, and it is thought that in these areas the land is between 12 and 13 ft. lower than it was in Roman times. The county's climate, however, boasts the lowest rainfall and the highest summer temperatures in Britain. The county's industries include boat-building and fishing, particularly for oysters, oil storage and refining, as well as agriculture.

MARKET TOWNS

Surprisingly, Southend is the county's largest town outside the London sprawl. There is no big industrial town. Chelmsford, the county town, has some light industry, mainly electronic. It also has a cathedral church, though it is not celebrated as such, because until 1913 it was the parish church.

Colchester, though not the county town, is in the words of Pevsner 'without any doubt the foremost town of Essex, and is a town richer than most in the country in traditions and survivals of a distant past. It was the Roman provincial capital of Camulodunum. After the Norman Conquest, William built a castle, and the surviving keep is said to be the largest in Europe. It is certainly bigger than London's White Tower.

There are many good churches, from Norman to Victorian. There are fine Georgian houses spread around the town, and the High Street offers a rare mixture of notable buildings from many centuries. Other notable towns are Braintree, Saffron Walden, the port of Harwich and the resorts of Frinton and Clacton-on-Sea; and there are the new towns of Basildon and Harlow, with prosperous light industry.

LEISURE

Essex offers some of the best sailing facilities within easy reach of London, both around Mersea Island and in the many tidal estuaries. There is hunting with the Essex, the East Essex, the Essex Farmers and the Essex and Suffolk. Among many golf courses are Boyce Hill, Clacton, Frinton and Maldon.

Chelmsford is the headquarters of Essex County Cricket Club, county champions in 1979, '83, '84 and '86.

GREAT HOUSES AND GARDENS

Among great houses the foremost is Audley End, in the care of English Heritage. Others are Hedingham Castle, with

(Below) **A typical Essex house with tiled roof and pargetting.**
(Top right) **A larger property in brick with stone facings.**
(Below right) **The Stour at Dedham: Constable country** *(Kenneth Scowen).*

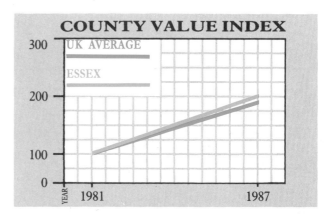

COUNTY VALUE INDEX

UK AVERAGE

ESSEX

300

200

100

0

1981   1987

YEAR

another great Norman keep; Saling Hall, near Braintree; and Layer Marney Tower, near Colchester. The National Trust has the merchant's house, Paycocke's, at Coggeshall, as well as 1,000 acres of Hatfield Forest on the Hertfordshire border.

Essex is one of the few counties that has retained its historic grammar schools. Essex County agricultural show is held at Great Leighs, Chelmsford, in mid-June.

COMMUNICATIONS

Train connections to Liverpool Street from:

Chelmsford, fastest travel time	40 mins
off-peak frequency	about 30 mins
Colchester, fastest travel time	52 mins
off-peak frequency	about 30 mins
Saffron Walden, fastest travel time	55 mins
off-peak frequency	about 1 hour

First commuter train to arrive in London at approximately 8.30 a.m.:

from Chelmsford	7.47 a.m.
from Colchester	7.31 a.m.
from Saffron Walden	7.15 a.m.

Road distances to central London from:

Chelmsford (via A12)	33 miles
Colchester (via A12)	57 miles
Saffron Walden (via M11)	40 miles

Airports: Road distances to:

	Heathrow	Gatwick
	(miles)	
Chelmsford	47	60
Colchester	71	84
Saffron Walden	54	67

	Stanstead	Southend
	(miles)	
Chelmsford	17	22
Colchester	32	44
Saffron Walden	13	46

HERTFORDSHIRE

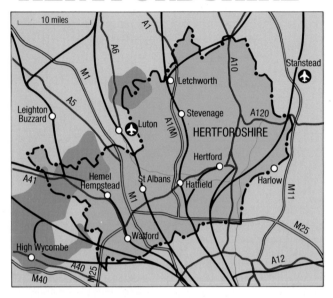

GEOGRAPHY

A relatively small county, Hertfordshire is densely populated, with the southern half being prime commuter territory. Immediately after the Second World War four New Towns were created to absorb some of London's increasing population. Recent development is associated with the M25, of which the last section in Hertfordshire was completed in 1986. The effect of this motorway has prompted commercial development (office and high tech) along its route through south Hertfordshire, particularly in the Hemel Hempstead, St Albans and Watford area. This new development has further emphasised the north-south contrast that exists within the county.

Hertfordshire is a county of arable land on which traditional crops of wheat and barley are grown. The countryside is gentle and intensively cultivated. There are three upland areas: in the south the London clay is heavily wooded; the northern area is boulder clay; while in the north-west, where it reaches towards the Chilterns, the land is predominantly chalk and Chiltern woodland, and is designated an Area of Outstanding Natural Beauty.

MARKET TOWNS

Hertford is one of the smallest county towns in England. Watford is the largest town. Other market towns include St Albans, Berkhamsted, Letchworth, Hitchin, Harpenden, Potters Bar, Cheshunt, Hoddesdon, Bishops Stortford and Royston. St Albans, once Verulamium, was one of the principal Roman towns in Britain, and much of it has been excavated. The part-Norman cathedral is magnificent, though Pevsner is unjustifiably impolite about it. The town is full of fine buildings, from medieval timber to Georgian and Victorian brick.

LEISURE

Golf courses are plentiful, indeed the game is almost a county industry, and range from Dyrham Park and Old Fold Manor, Barnet, to Moor Park, Rickmansworth. Foxhunting is with the Enfield Chase and the Puckeridge and Thurlow. The county agricultural show is held at Redbourn every year at the end of May.

GREAT HOUSES AND GARDENS

Great houses abound, as might be expected of a county so close to London. Most celebrated is Hatfield House, home of the Marquess of Salisbury. Others include Ashridge (now a management college), Knebworth House, Gorhambury House, home of the Earl of Verulam, and Moor Park Mansion, at Rickmansworth, now the headquarters of the golf club. In a different league is Shaw's Corner, Bernard Shaw's home at Ayot St Lawrence, now owned by the National Trust, which also has 4,000 acres of the Ashridge estate, including Ivinghoe Beacon.

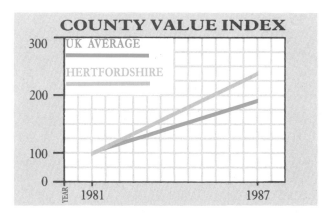

COUNTY VALUE INDEX

UK AVERAGE

HERTFORDSHIRE

(Far left) **A substantial Hertfordshire brick house.** *(Above, left)* **Rendered walls and tiled roofs.** *(Below, left)* **A fine property close to London.**

COMMUNICATIONS

 Train connections to King's Cross, Euston and Liverpool Street from:

Stevenage, fastest travel time	25 mins
off-peak frequency	3 per hr
Hemel Hempstead, fastest travel time	25 mins
off-peak frequency	2 per hr
Ware, fastest travel time	40 mins
off-peak frequency	2 per hr

First commuter train to arrive in London at approximately 8.30 a.m.:

from Stevenage	8.03 a.m.
from Hemel Hempstead	8.00 a.m.
from Ware	7.39 a.m.

 Approximate road distances to central London from:

Stevenage (via A1(M))	28 miles
Hemel Hempstead (via M1)	25 miles
Ware (via A10)	23 miles

 Airports: Approximate road distance from:

	Heathrow	Gatwick
	(miles)	
Stevenage	43	80
Hemel Hempstead	23	56
Ware	42	75

	Stanstead	Luton
	(miles)	
Stevenage	49	10
Hemel Hempstead	57	8
Ware	37	20

BUCKINGHAMSHIRE

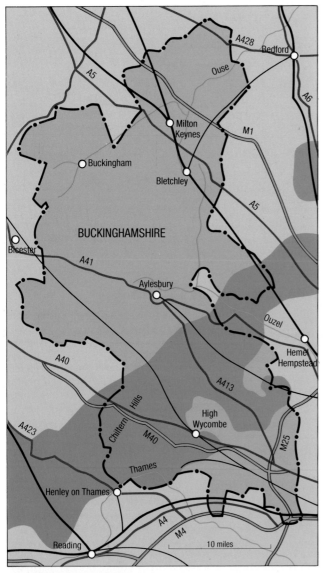

which have long supported a furniture industry centred on High Wycombe. Within living memory, craftsmen known as 'bodgers' turned the wood on primitive lathes. Burnham Beeches are the remnant of a native forest. The Thames Valley is exceptionally beautiful between Goring and Maidenhead, and Cliveden reach, with its hanging woods, is celebrated.

Because the southern part of the county is so close to London, it has offered a tempting target to building developers. Between the two World Wars, the management of the Metropolitan Railway made a deliberate effort to increase its traffic by promoting what became known as Metroland, and was celebrated by Betjeman, though the poet felt less warmly about one of the county's principal industrial towns — 'Come, friendly bombs, and fall on Slough, To get it ready for the plough'.

Since the inception of the Metropolitan Green Belt,

(Above) **A house embellished in the 18th-century.** *(Below)* **Classical symmetry.**

GEOGRAPHY

Buckinghamshire is an oddly shaped county, a narrow strip running north and south, with no natural boundary, except the Thames on its southern flank. That oddity, however, gives it one great advantage: an unusual variety of soil and scenery.

The chalk hills of the Chilterns divide the county in half, and present a steep escarpment to the north-west. Some of these hills run up to 800 ft. and more, offering wide views. Their south-eastern slope is more gentle and is broken by the valleys of the Wye, the Misbourn, the Chess and other chalk streams. The Chilterns are celebrated for their beeches, however, damaging development has been successfully checked, and most of the county remains unspoiled. Buckinghamshire happens to have had many connections with poets. Milton wrote part of *Paradise Lost* at Chalfont St Giles, where his cottage is now a museum; and Gray probably wrote his *Elegy* at Stoke Poges, where he is buried.

Agriculture has long been the principal source of the county's wealth, particularly in the fertile Vale of Aylesbury, though duck-fattening is no longer on the scale that gave culinary celebrity to Aylesbury ducks. Other market towns include Buckingham, Bletchley and Princes Risborough.

LEISURE

Local hunts are the Vale of Aylesbury, the Old Berkeley and the Whaddon Chase, now amalgamated with the Bicester. The Bucks County agricultural show is held at Hartwell Park, Aylesbury, in early September. Golf courses include

(Above) **A typical Buckinghamshire brick house.** *(Below)* **Variety of styles in West Wycombe** *(Kenneth Scowen).*

Gerrards Cross, Denham and Harewood Downs, near Chalfont St. Giles.

GREAT HOUSES AND GARDENS

Not surprisingly, a fertile county so close to the capital has more than its share of fine houses. Those within the care of the National Trust include Ascott House, near Leighton Buzzard, Claydon and Waddesdon, near Aylesbury, Cliveden, near Maidenhead, Hughenden (Disraeli's home), near High Wycombe and West Wycombe Park. The Trust also owns almost all the lovely village of West Wycombe. Other notable houses include Chicheley Hall near Newport Pagnell; Stowe, once the home of the Dukes of Buckingham; and Chequers, official home of the Prime Minister.

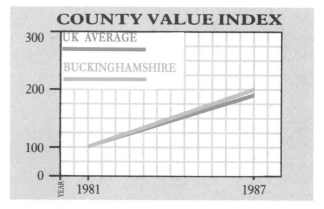

COMMUNICATIONS

 Train connections to Marylebone/Baker Street from:

High Wycombe, fastest travel time	45 mins
off-peak frequency	1 per hour
Aylesbury, fastest travel time	1 hr 15 mins
off-peak frequency	irregular
Milton Keynes, fastest travel time	35 mins
off-peak frequency	2 per hour

First commuter train to arrive in London at approximately 8.30 a.m.:
from High Wycombe   7.50 a.m.

 Road distances to central London from:

High Wycombe (via M40)	27 miles
Aylesbury (via A41[M])	36 miles
Buckingham (via A41)	53 miles

 Airports: Road distances to:

	Heathrow	Gatwick
	(miles)	
High Wycombe	28	46
Aylesbury	33	66
Buckingham	50	83

COUNTY VALUE INDEX

UK AVERAGE
BUCKINGHAMSHIRE

300
200
100
0
YEAR 1981 — 1987

OXFORDSHIRE

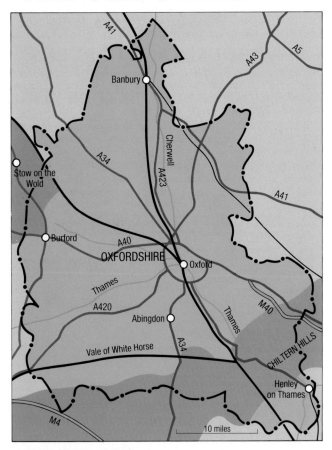

GEOGRAPHY

Although the Oxfordshire landscape may not be spectacular, it is most attractive. There remain many tracts of woodland, some of which, like Wychwood, are ancient relics of what once clothed the countryside. Contrast is provided by the watermeadows and marshland. Of the latter, Otmoor is the best known, an inland marsh that remained remote until the 19th century, with a drainage pattern which is said to have inspired Lewis Carroll's chess board in *Alice Through the Looking Glass.*

In the west, Oxfordshire claims part of the Cotswolds, with their gentle landscape of hill and valley interspersed with small villages. To the south-east lie the Chiltern Hills, a chalk escarpment that strides on into Buckinghamshire. This area, and that of the Cotswolds in the west, are both Areas of Outstanding Natural Beauty. Lying between them is the Vale of the White Horse, bounded by chalk hills that carry the cut-turf white horse and the Ridgeway, the oldest thoroughfare in the country, which is shared with Berkshire.

Agriculturally, Oxfordshire is one of the richest counties, with fertile mixed farmland and sheep rearing in the Cotswolds, and the celebrated Oxford Down sheep.

MARKET TOWNS

Oxford is the largest and richest town in the county, combining the roles of university city, county town and bishopric. For most of its history, until the arrival of industry in the present century, notably the Morris car factory at Cowley, the university was the dominant force in the city. Oxford grew up when the Saxons found an easy river crossing (Oxenford), but it enjoyed natural water defences within the encircling arms of the Isis (as the Thames is here called) and the Cherwell. The university is the oldest in Britain and one of the oldest in Europe.

In addition to its cultural and scholastic importance, the university has acquired an economic significance totally unpredictable until recently, in that it is now one of the primary attractions for overseas tourists in Britain. Other notable towns are Abingdon, Banbury, Bicester, Burford, Didcot, Henley-on-Thames, Thame, Wallingford, Watlington and Wantage.

LEISURE

Hunting is with the Bicester and Whaddon Chase, the Old Berkshire and the V.W.H. A great attraction, at the south-eastern corner of the county, is Henley Royal Regatta,

(Below) **Oxfordshire boasts many stone houses with slate or tiled roofs set in attractive gardens and landscape.**

Arable farming near Ewelme *(Kenneth Scowen).*

running from Wednesday to Sunday. Henley Saturday is traditionally the first Saturday in July. Among golf courses are the North Oxford, the Southfield and the Chesterton near Bicester.

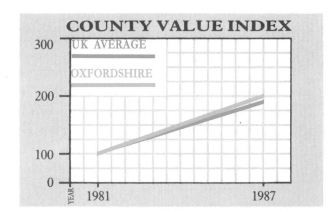

GREAT HOUSES AND GARDENS

Great houses in the county are dominated inevitably by Blenheim Palace, Vanbrugh's masterpiece built for the first Duke and Duchess of Marlborough. But there are many others, among them Broughton Castle, near Banbury; Kingstone Lisle near Wantage; and Ditchley Park, Enstone. National Trust properties include Greys Court, Henley-on-Thames; Buscot Park, Faringdon; and the great 13th-century barn at Great Coxwell.

Among notable schools is Radley, near Abingdon.

COMMUNICATIONS

 Train connections to Paddington from:

Oxford, fastest travel time	1 hour
off-peak frequency	1 per hour
Banbury, fastest travel time	1hr 25 mins
off-peak frequency	irregular
Henley-on-Thames, fastest travel time	50 mins
off-peak frequency	1 per hour

First commuter train to arrive in London at approximately 8.30 a.m.:

from Oxford	7.33 a.m.
from Banbury	6.35 a.m.
from Henley-on-Thames	7.30 a.m.

 Approximate road connections to central London from:

Oxford (via A40, M40)	57 miles
Banbury (via A423, A40, M40)	61 miles
Henley-on-Thames (via A423, M4)	28 miles

 Airports: approximate road distance from:

	Heathrow	Gatwick	Luton
		(miles)	
Oxford	43	80	42
Banbury	85	100	48
Henley-on-Thames	23	58	43

BERKSHIRE

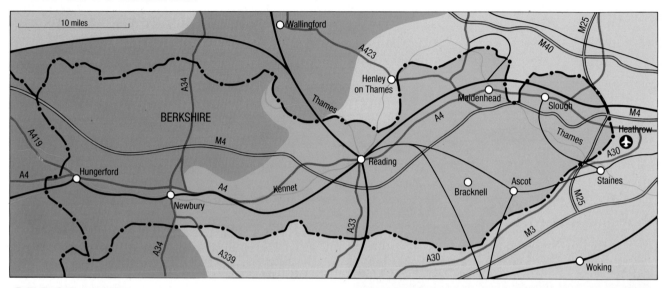

GEOGRAPHY

Anyone looking out from the tower of Windsor Castle, perched on its cliff above the Thames, commands a panoramic view of the Royal County of Berkshire. That county is now engaged in one of the most interesting and dramatic changes in its long history. There are three reasons for those changes — all of them as much concerned with ease of communication as was the original choice of Windsor as a royal residence, because of its easy route by river to London at all times of the year. First, there is the Great Western Railway, now Western Region of British Rail, but maintaining something of the romance and efficiency of Brunel's masterpiece. Then there is M4, with the easiest access of all London's radial motorways to the heart of the capital. Third, there is Heathrow, the world's busiest airport, alongside M4.

That remarkable combination of good communications has caused Berkshire to become the main centre of Britain's micro-electronics industry, among other industrial developments. What remains as yet uncertain is whether the new wealth that is flowing into the Royal County will bring the obvious advantages of high employment, or whether it will also bring with it the destructive effect on amenity that has accompanied new industries elsewhere in the past. In Berkshire's case, the auguries are good. The microchip and its accomplices are 'user friendly', so far as the environment is concerned. Moreover, the county is well protected by the planning system. Much of eastern Berkshire lies within the Metropolitan Green Belt. Similarly, a large part of western Berkshire lies within an Area of Outstanding Natural Beauty. Individual development therefore tends to be concentrated in the area bounded by the ancient town of Reading, with its young university, and the New Town of Bracknell. Other notable towns are Newbury, Maidenhead and Hungerford.

(Above) **Mature brickwork, dormer windows and stone facings.** *(Right)* **A typical Berkshire house in established gardens.**

(Above) **Wisteria on old brickwork.** *(Right)* **Great Shefford church set among the cornfields** *(Kenneth Scowen).*

BERKSHIRE

LEISURE

The landscape that is being protected is based partly on the Berkshire Downs with, among their more obvious amenities, Ascot racecourse to the east, and the prehistoric highway, known to us as the Ridgeway (another of the county's historic arteries of communication), running high along the chalk hills that are Berkshire's backbone.

GREAT HOUSES AND GARDENS

A county with such easy access to the Court of St James's has long attracted rich and powerful subjects of the Crown, but surprisingly little of Berkshire is owned by the National Trust, whose properties in the county, apart from Basildon Park, are based on landscape rather than architecture. Among historic houses open to the public are Swallowfield Park, near Reading, built by the second Earl of Clarendon in 1678.

Royal properties, however, tend to be dominant. There are Frogmore Gardens at Windsor, the Savill Gardens and the Valley Garden, adjoining Windsor Great Park, and of course Windsor Castle, one of the most loved and visited of all the historic houses in Britain. Alongside Windsor lies England's most famous public school, Eton.

Fox hunting is with the Old Berkshire, the Garth and South Berks and with Mr Goschen's. There are many golf-courses, among them the Berkshire, at Ascot; Calcot Park, Reading; and the East Berkshire at Crowthorne. There are many rowing clubs on the Thames, the most famous being Leander Club, on the Berkshire bank at Henley.

(Right) **Early-18th-century brickwork.** *(Far right)* **The Town Hall, Windsor** *(Kenneth Scowen).* *(Below)* **Timber-framing and Berkshire brick.** *(Below right)* **Market Cross House, Windsor** *(Kenneth Scowen).*

COUNTY VALUE INDEX

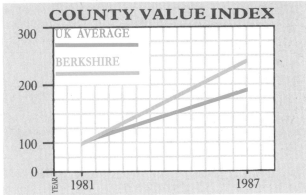

UK AVERAGE

BERKSHIRE

300

200

100

0

YEAR   1981   1987

COMMUNICATIONS

Train connections to Paddington from:

Newbury, fastest travel time	1 hr
off-peak frequency,	1 per hour
Reading, fastest travel time	22 mins
off-peak frequency	4 per hour

First commuter train to arrive in London at approximately 8.30 a.m.:

from Newbury	7.07 a.m.
from Reading	8.06 a.m.

Road distances to central London from:

Newbury (via M4)	60 miles
Reading (via M4)	44 miles

Airports: Approximate road distance from:

	Heathrow	Gatwick
	(miles)	
Newbury	45	82
Reading	30	67

SURREY

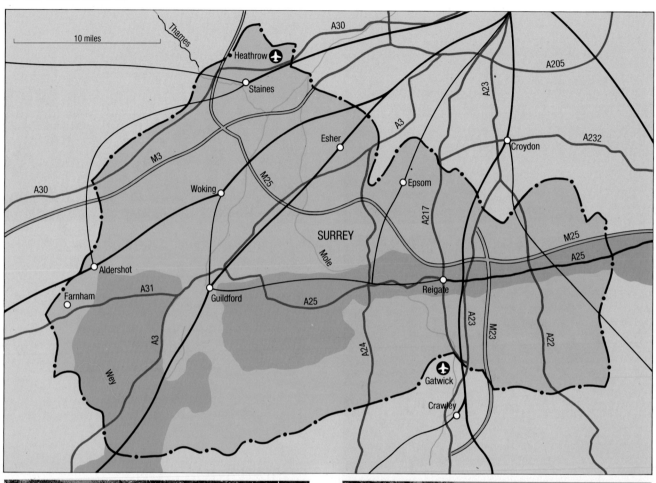

Heathrow
A30
A205
Thames
10 miles
Staines
M3
Esher
A3
A23
Croydon
A232
A30
Woking
M25
Epsom
A217
SURREY
M25
A25
Mole
Aldershot
A31
Farnham
A3
Guildford
A25
Reigate
A23
M23
A22
Wey
A24
Gatwick
Crawley

GEOGRAPHY

The survival of rural Surrey is something of a miracle. It is one of the smaller English counties, lying directly in the path of the expansion of London to the south-west. Yet much of the county remains agricultural and unspoiled, and it is exceptionally well-wooded. It was saved from urbanisation first by the establishment of the Metropolitan Green Belt and, more recently, by the protection given to the North Downs and other parts as Areas of Outstanding Natural Beauty. Yet Surrey has the easiest communications by road and rail to central London of any of the Home Counties, with the possible exception of Berkshire.

The northern edge of the county is bordered by the Thames; to the south is the Surrey end of the Weald — heavy clay that was once oak forest. Between lie the chalk of the North Downs and wide stretches of light, sandy soil, much of it heathland.

MARKET TOWNS

The county town of Surrey is still generally considered to be Guildford, the largest town in the county. But the situation is confused because, since the local government reorganisation of 1963, the administrative centre, with County Hall, has been at Kingston, which is not now in Surrey at all (though the Post Office still thinks it is), but in the Royal Borough of Kingston upon Thames, which is part of Greater London.

Guildford has retained much of its historic character and boasts a celebrated royal grammar school. Other notable towns are Bletchingley, Cobham, Cranleigh, Dorking, Farnham, Godalming, Horley, Oxted, Redhill and Reigate.

LEISURE

Surrey is celebrated for its racecourses, established there because of light, quick-draining soil. The most famous, of course, is at Epsom, but there are also Sandown Park and Lingfield. The light soil, and proximity to London, have favoured the establishment of golf-courses of which there are many, notably St George's Hill and Wentworth.

Foxhunting is offered by the Old Surrey and Burstow, with kennels at Felbridge, and the Surrey Union, with kennels near Ockley. The Union has a long history, dating from 1799.

GREAT HOUSES AND GARDENS

National Trust properties include Clandon Park, near Guildford, Ham House, near Richmond, and Polesden Lacey, near Dorking. Open country in the care of the Trust includes Box Hill and 700 acres of Leith Hill, both near Dorking. Other houses open to the public — and there are many in the county — include Loseley House near Guildford (Loseley is also widely known for its successful marketing of dairy products), Sutton Place, Guildford, and Greathed Manor near Lingfield. Many fine gardens open to the public include the Royal Horticultural Society's at Wisley.

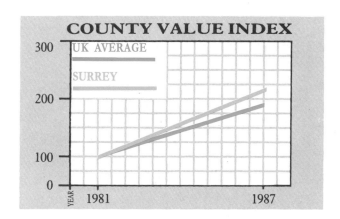

COUNTY VALUE INDEX

(Far left) **Autumn on Box Hill** *(Kenneth Scowen).*
(Left) **Surrey houses nestle deep in the landscape.**

COMMUNICATIONS

Train connections to Waterloo and Victoria from:

Guildford, fastest travel time	35 mins
off-peak frequency	2 per hour
Reigate, fastest travel time	36 mins
off-peak frequency	2 per hour
Godalming, fastest travel time	40 mins
off-peak frequency	2 per hour

First commuter train to arrive in London at approximately 8.30 a.m.:

from Guildford	7.40 a.m.
from Reigate	7.50 a.m.
from Godalming	7.47 a.m.

Approximate road distances to central London from:

Guildford (via A3)	31 miles
Reigate (via A23, (M23))	23 miles
Godalming (via A3)	35 miles

Airports: Approximate road distance from:

	Heathrow	Gatwick
	(miles)	
Guildford	23	24
Reigate	28	8
Godalming	27	23

KENT

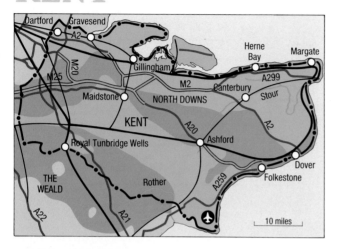

GEOGRAPHY

On paper, Kent is set to be the most prosperous county in England. Already the completion of the M25 has greatly improved its communications, especially in that it is no longer necessary to go through London to drive from Kent to Heathrow, or to the Midlands or the North. As a result, property values within easy reach of the M25 have risen sharply. The second influence on the economic future of Kent is its position nearest to the Continent. As Britain's trade links with the rest of the European Community continue to grow, more and more Continental firms are likely to establish bases in Kent. French firms, for example, are already choosing towns like Tunbridge Wells because of their amenities, coupled with their nearness to the Channel ports and to Gatwick airport. That influence can only increase when the Channel Tunnel is built.

The problem that must inevitably accompany the prosperity is how to prevent the urbanisation of a county that has so long boasted of being the Garden of England. Even without the influence of the Common Market, Kentish agriculture has changed. Fruit-growing is no longer so prosperous, and hop-growing has diminished with changing tastes in beer and with changing methods of brewing. Dairying and sheep farming have continued to prosper, in spite off the decline of the Kent or Romney Marsh breed in the face of competition from newer and more prolific breeds of sheep.

Kent's communications with London by rail have long been good, and the county has attracted rail commuters. Its road communications with the capital are weaker than Surrey's or Berkshire's, however, because its motorways and dual-carriageway roads stop far short of central London. Since the completion of the M25, it is sometimes quicker to drive from mid-Kent to central London via the M25 and the south-western access roads.

(Right) **Medieval timber-framing in Kent.**

MARKET TOWNS

In fine buildings and historic towns, Kent is as rich as any county in Britain. Dover's magnificent castle is unique in that it continued to serve a military purpose from the day it was built until the end of the Second World War. It was traditionally said that he who held the keys of Dover Castle held the keys of England. Canterbury Cathedral is only one attraction in a beautiful and historic town. To Canterbury can be added not only the prosperous commercial centres of Maidstone and Ashford, but such towns as Faversham and Sevenoaks, which have managed to preserve much of their original character in spite of their position as dormitory towns.

(Right) **Thatched cottage in Kent.**

(Above) **The Post Mill at Cranbrook** *(Kenneth Scowen).*
(Below) **Looking along the Pantiles in Tunbridge Wells**
(Kenneth Scowen).

LEISURE

Famous Kentish schools include Tonbridge School and Benenden. Local hunts include the West Kent, the East Kent, the Ashford Valley and the Tickham. Among celebrated golf courses are the Royal Cinque Ports at Deal and the Royal St George's at Sandwich. There is a notable course in the park at Knole. Kent is a great cricket county. The county ground is at Canterbury, famed for having a tree within the boundary. The history of the game in Kent dates back at least to 1709 at county level. Famous Kentish names include Frank Woolley, Les Ames and Colin Cowdrey, the latter a product of the celebrated 'Tonbridge Nursery'. Sailing facilities abound, on the Medway and on the Channel coast.

(Left) **Brick and slate in Kent.** *(Below)* **Stone and mellow brickwork.** *(Above, right)* **Clapboarding and a steep pitched roof.** *(Below)* **Apple blossom and a converted oasthouse** *(Kenneth Scowen).*

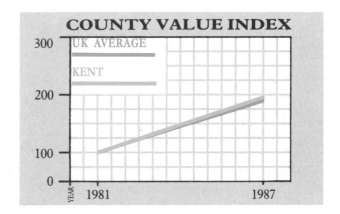

COUNTY VALUE INDEX

300	UK AVERAGE	
200	KENT	
100		
0		
YEAR	1981	1987

GREAT HOUSES AND GARDENS

The most renowned of Kentish great houses are Knole and Penshurst Place, both among the finest historic houses in Europe. The National Trust owns Knole, near Sevenoaks, with an ancient park, together with Quebec House, Westerham, Ightham Mote and Churchill's home, Chartwell, where he was able to indulge his leisure pursuits not only of painting but of bricklaying. Other notable houses are Leeds Castle, Maidstone, well-restored and retaining its fairy-tale quality; Hever Castle, Edenbridge; and Squerryes Court, Westerham. Among gardens open to the public are the National Trust's Sissinghurst, Crittenden House at Matfield and Hall Place at Leigh.

COMMUNICATIONS

Train connections to Victoria and Charing Cross from:

Canterbury, fastest travel time	1 hr 22 mins
off-peak frequency	1 per hour
Folkestone, fastest travel time	1 hr 30 mins
off-peak frequency	2 per hr
Maidstone, fastest travel time	1 hr
off-peak frequency	2 per hr

First commuter train to arrive in London at approximately 8.30 a.m.:

from Canterbury	7.00 a.m.
from Folkestone	6.39 a.m.
from Maidstone	7.20 a.m.

Road distances to central London from:

Canterbury (via A28)	58 miles
Folkestone (via M20)	66 miles
Maidstone (via M20)	32 miles

Airports: Approximate road distance from:

	Heathrow	Gatwick
	(miles)	
Canterbury	82	63
Folkestone	90	71
Maidstone	56	37

THE SOUTH

SUSSEX

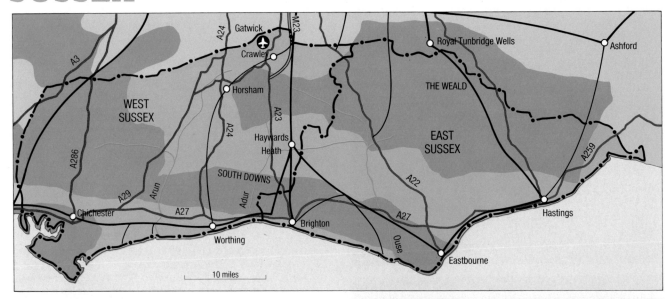

GEOGRAPHY

'Silly Sussex', as the phrase goes, has been anything but silly in the management of its affairs. It has generated great prosperity from its coastal assets — the national habit of sea-bathing virtually began at Brighton in Georgian days — and yet has succeeded in retaining the South Downs, unspoiled and sparsely populated, only a few miles behind the prosperous and densely populated coastal strip.

Administratively, Sussex is divided into two counties, East and West, but has retained its historical and traditional unity, each half sharing the county's characteristics of coastal strip, South Downs and, north of the Downs, the former oak forests of the Weald. Though most of the oak forest has gone and been replaced by agriculture, the Weald of Sussex is still richly wooded, as anyone can see who stands on the South Downs and looks north. It was that northern, wooded view that Kipling had in mind when he wrote of 'the dim, blue goodness of the Weald'.

MARKET TOWNS

It is indicative of the role that its coastline has played in the development of Sussex that Brighton is the county's largest town, followed by Worthing. Other important coastal towns are Hove, Hastings, Eastbourne, Bexhill, Bognor Regis, Seaford and Newhaven. The medieval walled town of Rye was once a coastal port, but has been some miles inland since the coast receded. Rye has succeeded in retaining its unique character in spite of its great attraction to tourists in the summer. The cathedral city of Chichester is rich in small

(Right) **Vernacular houses in Midhurst** *(Kenneth Scowen).* *(Top right)* **A typical Sussex house.** *(Below right)* **Period property in a mature garden.**

SUSSEX

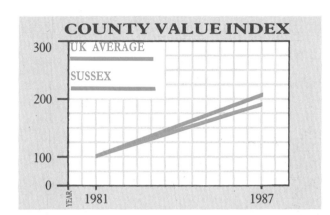

COUNTY VALUE INDEX

UK AVERAGE

SUSSEX

(Top left) **Stone and timber-framing in Sussex.** *(Below left)* **Arundel Castle above the Arun** *(Kenneth Scowen).* *(Above)* **The gardens of Glyndebourne** *(Kenneth Scowen).*

18th-century houses. Inland towns include Haywards Heath, Horsham, East Grinstead, the new town of Crawley with its strong industrial base alongside the international airport at Gatwick, Billingshurst and the beautiful hill-town of Lewes, exceptionally rich in small 18th-century and early-19th-century town houses.

LEISURE

Among local packs of foxhounds are the Crawley and Horsham, and the Southdown and Eridge. For those who ride but do not hunt, Sussex offers a wide variety of good riding country with many equestrian centres, among them the celebrated Crabbet Park, at Worth, near Crawley.

Among golf courses, one of the most celebrated is at Rye. The main agricultural show is the South of England Show, held at Ardingly in early June. Facilities for coastal sailing abound, in natural harbours and at Chichester and in new marinas at coastal resorts.

GREAT HOUSES AND GARDENS

The attraction of living in Sussex, for those who can afford it, has been well understood since Roman times; the remains of the great palace at Fishbourne is only one of many surviving ruins of luxurious Roman houses in the county. Fine country houses still survive from Elizabethan, Jacobean and Georgian times.

Among National Trust properties are Kipling's home, Bateman's, near Etchingham, Lamb House in Rye, and the magnificent moated Bodiam Castle, restored (but not to habitable standard) by Lord Curzon. Great houses open to the public abound. Notable among them are Firle Place and Glynde Place, near Lewes, Great Dixter at Northiam, Michelham Priory near Hailsham, Goodwood House and Arundel Castle.

COMMUNICATIONS

Train connections to Victoria from:

Brighton, fastest travel time	55 mins
off-peak frequency	2 per hour
Crawley, fastest travel time	40 mins
off-peak frequency	3 per hour
Chichester, fastest travel time	1 hr 40 mins
off-peak frequency	1 per hour

First commuter train to arrive in London at approximately 8.30 a.m.:

from Brighton	7.16 a.m.
from Crawley	7.47 a.m.
from Chichester	7.18 a.m.

Approximate road distances to central London from:

Brighton (via A23, M23)	50 miles
Crawley (via M23)	31 miles
Chichester (via A27, A29, A241, A3)	71 miles

Airports: Approximate road distances from:

	Heathrow	Gatwick
	(miles)	
Brighton	46	23
Crawley	27	4
Chichester	58	44

HAMPSHIRE

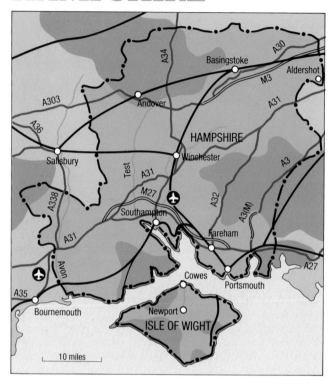

GEOGRAPHY

Though Berkshire is officially the 'Royal' county (because of Windsor), Hampshire has an older claim to that title. Winchester was the original capital of the Kings of Wessex, including Alfred the Great. Little is left of William the Conqueror's palace at Winchester, but the New Forest is still a reminder that the Norman rulers' favourite hunting ground was in the heavily wooded southern part of the county.

Winchester's predominance did not long survive in the era of Norman rule. The road from London to the county became known not as the Winchester road but as the Portsmouth road, because of the dominance of Portsmouth as a seaport and naval base. It was rivalled by Southampton, which remained the major south coast port until much of Europe's container traffic moved to Rotterdam. When the Channel Tunnel is built, and Southampton has direct rail links with the Continent, it may recover something of its old supremacy, as the European terminal for Atlantic shipping. The uplands of north Hampshire rise to 700 ft. and have rounded hills and deep valleys typical of chalk country. South of the chalk a low plateau slopes gently to the sea.

MARKET TOWNS

Notable towns include Alton, Basingstoke, Brockenhurst, Fareham, Havant, Petersfield and Romsey. The most famous of the county's schools is Winchester College.

LEISURE

The tradition of hunting has continued since Norman times. Notable packs of hounds are the 'H.H.' (Hampshire Hounds), the Hursley Hambledon, and the New Forest. The Forest is also hunted by the New Forest Buckhounds.

Among fishermen, Hampshire is celebrated for its chalk streams, notably the Test and the Itchen. The current edition of *Where to Fish* says of the Test: 'Before the era of the rainbow, the brown trout Mecca of the whole civilised world. Now considered by some to have been spoilt to some degree by the introduction of the former'.

Golf courses include the Royal Winchester. Partridge shooting has traditionally been good in Hampshire, though

A classical Hampshire house: red brick, glazing bars and dormer windows. *(Below)* **The Test near Whitchurch** *(Kenneth Scowen).*

bags have fallen with the general decline in partridge numbers. They now show signs of revival. The Game Conservancy, which has done so much to establish the reasons for the decline in the partridge and to encourage its recovery, has its headquarters at Fordingbridge, in Hampshire. Romsey agricultural show is held in the park at Broadlands in early September.

GREAT HOUSES AND GARDENS

Winchester Cathedral, Romsey Abbey and Christchurch Priory are among the county's most distinguished churches. Its many great houses include Beaulieu (now celebrated also for its National Motor Museum), Broadlands (home of Earl

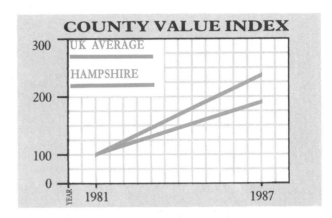

The Itchen at Abbots Worthy *(Kenneth Scowen).* *(Below)* **Tile-hanging and brick in the Itchen valley.**

Mountbatten) and the Elizabethan Breamore House, near Fordingbridge. National Trust properties include Mottisfont Abbey, near Romsey, and The Vyne, near Basingstoke. The Trust also owns the hanging beech-woods above Selborne, near Alton, celebrated in Gilbert White's *Natural History of Selborne*. Among other Hampshire writers is Jane Austen, whose home at Chawton, near Selborne, is open to the public. *Mansfield Park, Emma* and *Persuasion* were written there, and it was there that Jane revised *Pride and Prejudice* and *Sense and Sensibility*.

COMMUNICATIONS

Train connections to Waterloo from:

Southampton, fastest travel time	1 hr 13 mins
off-peak frequency	About 30 mins
Portsmouth, fastest travel time	1 hour 30 mins
off-peak frequency	About 30 mins
Basingstoke, fastest travel time	48 mins
off-peak frequency	About 45 mins

First commuter train to arrive in London at approximately 8.30 a.m.:

from Southampton	6.55 a.m.
from Portsmouth	6.49 a.m.
from Basingstoke	7.40 a.m.

Road distances to central London from:

Southampton (via M3)	80 miles
Portsmouth (via A3[M], M3)	74 miles
Basingstoke (via M3)	48 miles

Airports: road distances to:

	Heathrow	Gatwick
	(miles)	
Southampton	65	53
Portsmouth	60	51
Basingstoke	33	21

Southampton has scheduled flights to: Aberdeen (1 to 5 per day); Guernsey (1 to 7 per day); Jersey (1 per day); Amsterdam (2 per day).

COUNTY VALUE INDEX

UK AVERAGE

HAMPSHIRE

300

200

100

0

YEAR 1981 1987

THE WEST

GLOUCESTERSHIRE AND AVON

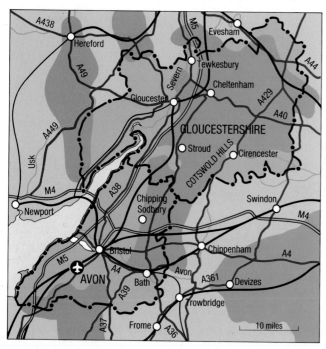

GEOGRAPHY

Gloucestershire people claim that the county has two distinct geographical personalities. The Cotswold hills form one; the gentler Severn valley and the Forest of Dean make up the other.

The Cotswolds are designated an Area of Outstanding Natural Beauty. The central area of Gloucestershire, primarily consisting of the Vale of Berkeley, is a landscape of dairyland and orchards. The second of the county's two personalities is to be found in the west. The Severn valley is a fertile region, with the major towns of Gloucester and Cheltenham. The nearby Forest of Dean has been described as 'The most beautiful assembly of trees in England'. It is unlike any other part of Gloucestershire, with a quality akin to childhood concepts of fairytale forests. In parts, it contains remnants of the ancient prehistoric forest.

Avon too, has part of the Cotswold Area of Outstanding Natural Beauty in the north east, less dramatic here than it is further north. Another AONB is the Mendip plateau, the fringe of which forms a natural boundary.

The northern heartland is an area of gentle, rural relief. Around the Severn shore is flat clay or peat moorland. The coastline does possess some stretches of sand, notably at Weston bay, but these are not extensive. The southern

(Top right) **Gloucestershire landscape near Upper Slaughter** *(Kenneth Scowen)*. *(Right)* **Stone house typical of Gloucestershire.** *(Far right)* **The West Front of Bath Abbey** *(Kenneth Scowen)*.

heartland, including the Avon valley, presents a variety of scenery, from marshland to pastures, with small villages and hamlets, to lakes and reservoirs. The two major industrial and manufacturing areas are in the north-west. Generally, the county escaped the worst impact of the Industrial Revolution.

Both counties were subject to Roman rule, which endowed them with the Fosse Way and some of their first major urban developments, such as the Roman spa at Bath, from which the city derives its name. Most of the villages of Avon can be identified in Domesday, and Gloucestershire contains some of the most important Saxon remains in the country, at Deerhurst.

MARKET TOWNS

Bristol is the largest city within Avon, and other towns are Bath, Keynsham, Nailsea, Yate, Radstock and Chipping Sodbury. On the coast are Clevedon, Portishead and Weston-super-Mare.

GLOUCESTERSHIRE AND AVON

In Gloucestershire, the largest communities are Gloucester and Cheltenham. Other towns are Newent, Tewkesbury, Stroud, Anderford and Dursley.

LEISURE

Gloucestershire is the home of one of the older and most distinguished of English hunts — the Duke of Beaufort's. *Baily's Hunting Directory* says of it: 'A horse that can go fast, stay, and jump every sort of fence is required.' Other packs are the Berkeley and the Ledbury. The kennels of the Duke of Beaufort's are at Badminton, now equally-renowned in the horse world for its annual three-day event.

There is flat racing at Bath from April to October and National Hunt racing at Cheltenham from October to April. A wide range of fishing is offered by the Avon and its many tributaries, while Gloucestershire's streams include the Frome. There is an abundant choice of golf courses, among them Painswick, near Stroud, Lydney, Minchinhampton, and Strinchcombe, near Dursley.

GREAT HOUSES AND GARDENS

National Trust properties include Newark Park, at Wotton-under-Edge; Snowshill Manor, Broadway; Hidcote Garden, near Chipping Campden; and Westbury Court Garden, at Westbury-on-Severn; and Dyrham Park, near Bath. Other houses open to the public include Berkeley Castle, Sudeley Castle, Spanway House and Kiftsgate Court, near Chipping Campden.

Agricultural shows include the Royal Bath and West, at Shepton Mallet, at the end of May.

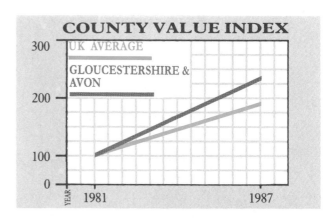

COUNTY VALUE INDEX

UK AVERAGE

GLOUCESTERSHIRE & AVON

(Far left) **Cotswold stone with gables in a steep pitched roof.**
(Left) **Tewkesbury from the Abbey Gateway** (Kenneth Scowen). (Below) **Stone house of the classical period.**

COMMUNICATIONS

Train connections to Paddington from:
Bristol, fastest travel time   1 hr 30 mins
    off-peak frequency   1 per hr
Cheltenham, fastest travel time   1 hr 52 mins
    off-peak frequency   1 per hr
Cirencester (Kemble), fastest travel time
                 1 hr 6 mins
    off-peak frequency   1 per hr
First commuter train to arrive in London at approximately 8.30 a.m.;
from Bristol   6.55 a.m.
from Cheltenham   6.12 a.m.
from Cirencester   6.58 a.m.

Approximate road distances to central London from:
Bristol (via M4)   119 miles
Cheltenham (via A40, M40)   120 miles
Cirencester (via A419, M4)   92 miles

Airports: Approximate road distance from:

	Heathrow	Gatwick
	(miles)	
Bristol	104	151
Cheltenham	106	153
Cirencester	77	124

Regional: Bristol airport which has scheduled flights to:
Amsterdam, 2 per day (Mon.-Fri.)
Dublin, 1 to 2 per day
Jersey, 3 per week

HEREFORD AND WORCESTERSHIRE

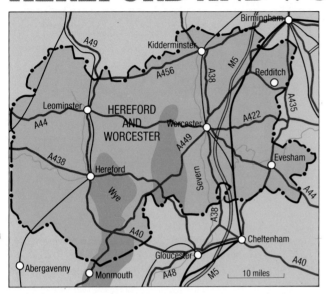

GEOGRAPHY

Until the government reorganisation of 1974, Hereford and Worcestershire were separate, adjoining counties. Their geographical characters are quite similar, both having areas of lowland surrounded by hills.

Hereford's lowland is composed of rich river valleys of fertile redstone soil. Hereford cattle have a world-wide fame, and the county's sheep have also been important. This central plain is primarily agricultural, and has changed little in appearance over the past few hundred years. Parts of it remain wooded, including the Royal Forest of Dean, and there are numerous orchards.

The Black Mountains lie in the south west, containing the highest point in England south of Yorkshire. Due south are the Old Red Sandstone hills, and in the east the Malverns, an Area of Outstanding Natural Beauty.

Worcestershire also contains part of the Malvern Hills, rising in its western landscape. The other major upland area is the Clent and Lickey Hills in the north east. As with neighbouring Hereford, Worcestershire is predominantly rural. The only coal deposits are in the extreme south west (south east of Hereford). Neither county had a mineral resource to exploit during the Industrial Revolution, and consequently each escaped with few of the scars that are often associated with it.

Sauce is one product that has made Worcestershire a household name, even to those who have never visited the county. It is also proud of its cricket, and claims to have, as the backdrop to its county matches, some of England's most beautiful scenery. The main rivers are the Wye, whose valley is an Area of Outstanding Natural Beauty, in Herefordshire, and the Terne and Severn in Worcestershire. Proximity to

Wales and constant fear of attack led to the building of a large number of castles in Herefordshire. Neither county was ever wealthy, and that is reflected in a lack of stately homes.

MARKET TOWNS

Hereford and Worcester are the two most important cities. Market towns are Droitwich, Great Malvern, Leominster, Kidderminster, Stourport, Bromyard, Kington and Ledbury.

LEISURE

Foxhunting is with the North Herefordshire, the South Herefordshire, the Radnorshire and West Herefordshire, and the Ledbury. There is National Hunt racing at Ludlow, Worcester and Hereford. Fishing waters include the Wye and its tributaries, and the Severn and tributaries.

Golf is at Droitwich Golf and Country Club, at

Evesham, at Habberley, at Kington and at Kidderminster, among many other courses in the counties.

GREAT HOUSES AND GARDENS

National Trust properties include Croft Castle and Berrington Hall, near Leominster, Hanbury Hall, near Droitwich, and the moated manor house of Lower Brockhampton near Bringsty, besides several areas of open countryside. Other properties open to the public include Abberley Hall, near Worcester; Bredon Springs, near Evesham; Dinmore Manor, near Hereford; Eastnor Castle, near Ledbury; Kentchurch Court, near Hereford, Little Malvern Court, near Great Malvern, the Priory at Kemerton, and Spatchley Park, near Worcester.

The Three Counties agricultural show is held in mid-June at Malvern, in one of the most beautifully sited of all showgrounds.

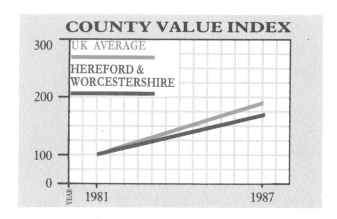

(Far left) **Black and white in Church Lane, Ledbury** *(Kenneth Scowen)* *(Left)* **The Wye at Symonds Yat** *(Kenneth Scowen).* *(Below)* **Typical Herefordshire house with Gothic windows.**

COMMUNICATIONS

 Train connections to Paddington from:

Hereford, fastest travel time	2 hrs 55 mins
off-peak frequency	1 per hr
Worcester, fastest travel time	2 hrs
off-peak frequency	1 per hr
Evesham, fastest travel time	1 hr 47 mins
off-peak frequency	irregular

First commuter train to arrive in London at approximately 8.30 a.m.:

from Hereford	6.00 a.m.
from Worcester	6.50 a.m.
from Evesham	7.06 a.m.

 Approximate road distances to central London from:

Hereford (via A49, A40, M40)	135 miles
Worcester (via M5, A40, M40)	120 miles
Evesham (via A10, A40, M40)	105 miles

 Airports: Approximate road distance from:

	Heathrow	Gatwick
	(miles)	
Hereford	120	167
Worcestershire	105	152
Evesham	90	137

Also close to Birmingham airport that has 27 international departures and scheduled flights to:
Heathrow, 3 to 6 per day
Gatwick, 1 to 3 per day

WILTSHIRE

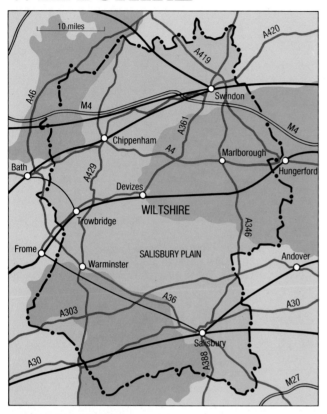

(Above) **Poultry Cross, Salisbury** *(Kenneth Scowen).*
(Right) **Old houses near the church in Marlborough** *(Kenneth Scowen).*

GEOGRAPHY

Wiltshire is typical English chalk country, with Salisbury Plain and the Marlborough Downs to the centre and north of the county. The population distribution is based on the rivers and the low-lying land around them, where there are many peaceful and secluded valleys within convenient reach of main roads. In the north-west of the county is an area of limestone overlaid with clay. Part of the Cotswolds, this area is not particularly high, but, towards Bath, there is some plateau and valley landscape. This is 'cow country', famed for its cheese.

The two main rivers, running north-south, are the Bristol Avon and the Salisbury Avon, providing a pleasant contrast in landscape to the Downs. Others are the Thames and Kennet, both good fishing rivers. Large areas of Salisbury Plain are used as a training ground by the army, but some public access remains. The Plain is classified as an Area of Outstanding Natural Beauty and is the largest expanse of chalk grassland in England.

The main woodland areas within the county are to the south-west, towards Somerset and Dorset. The south-east borders the New Forest, and the wooded areas of the south-west are part of the ancient Great Ridge Wood. Overall, this is a rural county, with small towns, Swindon being the only industrial centre.

Wiltshire is one of the richest counties in England in pre-historic remains. The monumental splendour of Stonehenge is an obvious example, but there are also Avebury, Windmill Hill, and the innumerable barrows of Salisbury Plain.

MARKET TOWNS

Swindon, placed in a convenient position between Bristol and London, was chosen by David Gooch as the site of the locomotive and carriage works of the Great Western Railway, opened in 1843. Its subsequent development led to the rapid growth of the town.

Salisbury, in spite of the incursion of motor traffic and inadequately bypassed, remains one of the most delightful towns in England, centred on its fine market-place and superb cathedral, which is renowned throughout the world for its spire, the tallest in England at 404 ft. It is, of course, equally famous for Constable's view of it across the water-meadows, but, like Exeter, it is rare among English cathedral churches in being, architecturally, all-of-a-piece —

WILTSHIRE

almost pure Early English. It survived ruthless 'restoration' by Wyatt at the beginning of the 19th century, compounded by an attempt by Scott to undo the Wyatt damage in the middle of the 19th century.

Other notable towns are Andover, Calne, Chippenham, Devizes, Malmesbury, Marlborough (with its distinguished public school), Trowbridge, Warminster and Westbury.

LEISURE

Wiltshire is a great sporting county: excellent shooting, fishing in its many chalk streams, and the full spectrum of horse activities, from three-day eventing to racing (at Salisbury) and from hacking over the chalk downs to hunting with the South and West Wilts, the Wilton, the R.A. Salisbury Plain, the Avon Vale and other packs. Though Wiltshire is not primarily a golfing county, there are many good courses, notably Marlborough, North Wiltshire and Salisbury and South Wilts. The principal local agricultural show, though not in the county, is the Bath and West, at Shepton Mallet.

GREAT HOUSES AND GARDENS

There is a profusion of historic houses. The National Trust have Lacock Abbey (where photography was invented) together with most of the village; Mompesson House in Salisbury Close; Stourhead with its great gardens, near Warminster; and Westwood Manor at Bradford-on-Avon. In private hands and open to the public, are, amongst others, Avebury Manor; Bowood, near Calne; Longleat, near Warminster; and the superb Wilton House with its famous double-cube room, near Salisbury.

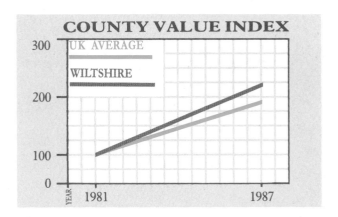

COUNTY VALUE INDEX

UK AVERAGE

WILTSHIRE

300
200
100
0

YEAR 1981 1987

(Far left) **A typical Georgian brick house in Wiltshire.**
(Left) **A unique property set in its own parkland.**

COMMUNICATIONS

Train connections to central London from:

Swindon, fastest travel time	50 mins
off-peak frequency	2 per hour
Chippenham, fastest travel time	1 hour 7 mins
off-peak frequency	1 per hour
Salisbury, fastest travel time	1 hour 24 mins
off-peak frequency	1 per hour

First commuter train to arrive in London at
 approximately 8.30 a.m.:

from Swindon	7.23 a.m.
from Chippenham	7.19 a.m.
from Salisbury	6.40 a.m.

Road connections to central London from:

Swindon (via M4)	76 miles
Chippenham (via M4)	93 miles
Salisbury (via A30, M3)	85 miles

Airports: Road distances from:

	Heathrow	Gatwick
	(miles)	
Swindon	62	93
Chippenham	78	108
Salisbury	70	90

Bristol Airport is also nearby and has scheduled
 flights to:
Amsterdam, 2 per day, Monday to Friday
Dublin, 1 to 2 per day
Jersey, 3 per week

SOUTH WEST

SOMERSET AND DORSET

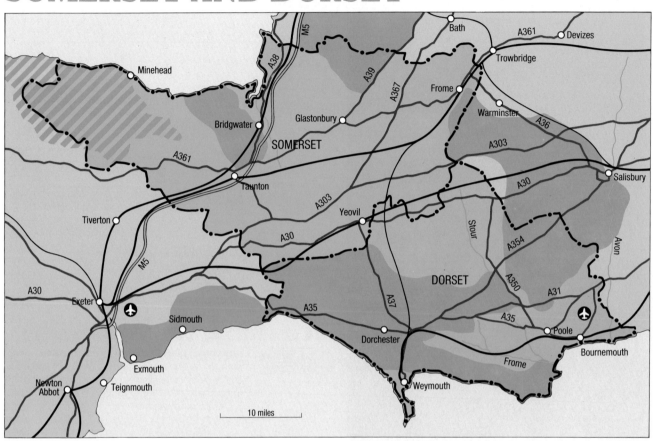

GEOGRAPHY

Both Somerset and Dorset contain scenery of great variety and beauty. Both include Areas of Outstanding Natural Beauty, and in Somerset lies the Exmoor National Park. Somerset's extremes of landscape range from the wilds of Exmoor to the crags of the Cheddar Gorge and the low wetlands of Sedgemoor. The south-east of the county is a gentle plain, rising in the north to the Quantock Hills. Farmland merges with heather moorland, together with wooded combes and forestry plantations, and it is all ringed by a series of picturesque villages. This was one of the first Areas of Outstanding Natural Beauty to be established.

Dorset can be roughly divided into three parts. First are the chalk uplands that dominate the landscape in the central part of the county. Second are the vales of the west and north-west, a gentle and fertile land of rivers and pasture. Third are the heaths and marshes of the south-east. The coastline of Dorset has some spectacular scenery and is of particular geological interest, with Chesil Beach, Lulworth

(Right) **The Old Yarn Market, Dunster, Somerset** *(Kenneth Scowen).*

(Above) **Classical stone house in Somerset.**
(Left) **Corfe Castle, Dorset** *(Kenneth Scowen).*

Cove and Portland Bill. Building stone is plentiful, and, indeed, St Paul's Cathedral is one of many London landmarks built of Portland stone from Dorset.

Dorset has been little affected by industry during any period in its history. There are some industrial landscapes, but these are fairly localised, among them quarrying and textiles. Despite the expansion of suburbia around most of Dorset's larger towns, the beauty and history of its landscape has remained. Thomas Hardy was born here and the Wessex novels are set mainly in Dorset.

MARKET TOWNS

Taunton is the county town of Somerset, and other notable towns are Bridgwater, Yeovil, Glastonbury, Wells, Shepton Mallet, Minehead, Wellington, Crewkerne and Frome.

Dorset's county town is Dorchester, while other notable towns are Poole, Bournemouth, Weymouth, Blandford, Bridport, Sherborne, Christchurch, Swanage, Wareham and Wimborne. Schools include Sherborne and Bryanston in Dorset, and Millfield in Somerset.

SOMERSET AND DORSET

LEISURE

All the principal field sports are available in profusion. Somerset offers foxhunting with the Exmoor, the Dulverton (East), the Dulverton (West), the West Somerset, the West Somerset Vale and the Taunton Vale. There is staghunting with the Devon and Somerset, with kennels at Exford. Dorset has four celebrated packs of foxhounds, the Blackmore Vale (now joined with the Sparkford Vale), the Portman, the Cattistock and the South Dorset.

Dorset offers a variety of fishing, with a fly-fishing centre, Wessex Fly-fishing, at Tolpuddle. Somerset is equally well provided with many streams, lakes and reservoirs. There is National Hunt racing in Somerset at Wincanton and Taunton, with fixtures over seven months. The many golf courses include Burnham and Berrow, Clevedon and Enmore Park (Bridgwater), in Somerset; and Came Down (Dorchester), Isle of Purbeck and Lyme Regis, in Dorset. The coastlines of both counties offer sailing, notably from Poole Harbour in Dorset.

GREAT HOUSES AND GARDENS

The National Trust is particularly strong in Dorset. It owns the immense Bankes estates, including Kingston Lacy House and Corfe Castle. Along the coast its properties include Brownsea Island, Studland beach, Ballard Down and the Golden Cap estate. Recent acquisitions in the county are Fontmell Down and Hod Hill. In Somerset, the Trust owns Barrington Court, near Ilminster; Dunster Castle, near

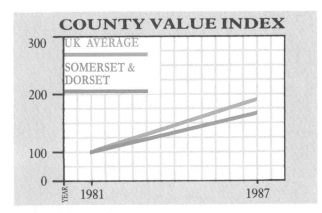

COUNTY VALUE INDEX

UK AVERAGE

SOMERSET & DORSET

(values on vertical axis: 300, 200, 100, 0; horizontal axis labelled YEAR with 1981 and 1987)

Minehead; and the 16th-century Montacute House, near Yeovil. English Heritage controls Portland Castle and Sherborne Old Castle. Other great houses open to the public include Athelhampton, Parnham, Sherborne Castle, Wolfeton and Milton Abbey. Notable gardens include Compton Acres, at Bournemouth, and Cranborne Manor Gardens, near Wimborne.

In Somerset, the great houses open to the public include the Bishop's Palace, in Wells, Brympton d'Evercy, near Yeovil, and Hatch Court, near Taunton.

COMMUNICATIONS

Train connections to Paddington and Waterloo from:

Taunton, fastest travel time	1 hr 55 mins
off-peak frequency	1 per 2 hrs
Weymouth, fastest travel time	2 hrs 45 mins
off-peak frequency	1 per hr
Bournemouth, fastest travel time	1 hr 40 mins
off-peak frequency	2 per hr

First commuter train to arrive in London at approximately 8.30 a.m.:

from Bournemouth	6.16 a.m.

Approximate road distances to central London from:

Taunton (via A303, M3)	148 miles
Weymouth (via M3)	145 miles
Bournemouth (via M3)	110 miles

Airports: Approximate road distance from:

	Heathrow	Gatwick
	(miles)	
Taunton	135	140
Weymouth	115	130
Bournemouth	80	92

Regional; Bournemouth: Scheduled flights to:

Guernsey 1 to 2 per day
Jersey 1 to 4 per day

(Left) **West Sedgemoor, Somerset** *(Kenneth Scowen).*
(Above) **An early stone house in Dorset.**

DEVON AND CORNWALL

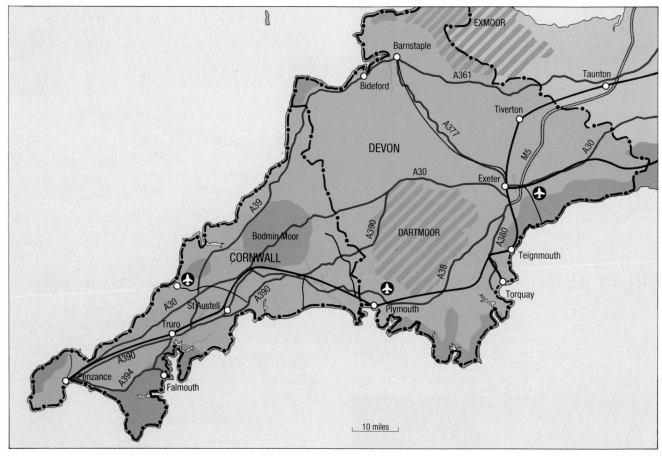

GEOGRAPHY

Devon and Cornwall are the most maritime of English counties. They are unique in sharing an Atlantic coast as well as a Channel coast, and the sea has dominated both their histories. They also share the mildest climate in Britain, with early springs and long summers. Yet in many aspects the two counties are surprisingly different. It used to be said: 'Cross the Tamar and you are in a foreign land'. Until recent centuries, Cornishmen retained their own language, akin to Welsh and Breton, and remained a race apart, though conquered in turn by Saxon and Norman rulers.

Even in the 1980s the sea remains the dominating influence, though maritime trade has declined, and smuggling, piracy and wrecking no longer contribute to the economy. The joint permanent population is only about 1½ million (it increases greatly in the summer), roughly two-thirds of them in Devon, sharing a land area of some 4,000 square miles divided in roughly the same ratio; but no inhabitant of Devon lives more than 25 miles from the sea, and in Cornwall that distance is down to 18 miles. The sea still brings in the money, but in a new way: tourism in both

counties shares with agriculture the status of principal industries.

Fortunately the coastline is still largely unspoilt, and is one of the most beautiful and variable in Europe, ranging from the sunlit bays and estuaries of the south to the rugged cliffs of the north.

A footpath of some 450 miles leads round the coast, offering walking that is rewarding but exhausting, because of the frequent and steep climbs and descents. About one-third of the coast of the two counties is already in the safe hands of the National Trust, which is steadily adding to its ownership. The uplands of Dartmoor and Exmoor enjoy similar protection as National Parks (the latter is partly in Somerset).

In both counties, the tumbling hills have protected local agriculture from the changes that have transformed the farmed landscape in some other regions. Farms are still small or medium-sized, and are therefore family farms; and though grain is grown over the granite of parts of Cornwall, and on the red sandstone of some of the Devon valleys, stock-raising has always been more profitable. High rainfall, and a long grass-growing season have particularly favoured dairying, an

advantage still reflected in the farmhouse production of Cornish or Devonshire cream, which, though differently named, is made by the same 'scalding' process.

Both counties are rich in prehistoric remains, notably on Dartmoor, reminders of a time when the moorlands probably enjoyed a more benign climate. The Romans left little mark in Cornwall, and in Devon mainly east of the Exe. Exeter, or Isca, is the only Roman city.

Exeter, the county town of Devon, is not only one of the most beautiful of English cities but one of the most civilised. At the heart of it lies the magnificent cathedral, rare among English cathedral churches in that it dates predominantly from one period, the 90 years following 1275. There is also the remains of a great castle, Rougemont, and a modern university with an exceptionally attractive campus and a growing reputation.

(Above) **Looking down to Widecombe on Dartmoor** *(Kenneth Scowen).* *(Right)* **Timber-framing in Devon.**

DEVON AND CORNWALL

MARKET TOWNS

The counties contain many historic towns. Notable in South Devon are Kingsbridge, Totnes, Newton Abbot, Plymouth, Brixham and Torquay. In the north are the rival towns of Barnstaple and Bideford. At the northern edge of Dartmoor is Okehampton, where the quality of daily life will be much improved by the completion of its long-awaited by-pass.

Cornwall has no city equivalent to Exeter. The ancient town of Bodmin remains technically the county town, but the administrative and ecclesiastical centre is effectively Truro, at the tidal head of the Fal. The cathedral, though built on the site of a 16th-century church, is of the 19th and 20th centuries.

LEISURE

Both counties have important agricultural shows, reflecting the primary role of farming in their economies. Devon County Show is held annually in late spring at its own ground at Whipton, near Exeter. The Royal Cornwall Show is held in early summer at its own ground at Wadebridge.

The principal race-courses in Devon are at Exeter (Haldon) and at Newton Abbot, with meetings nearly all the year round, under National Hunt rules. Among the principal yacht clubs are the Royal Western at Plymouth, the Royal Plymouth Corinthian, the Mayflower Sailing Club at Plymouth, the Royal Dart at Dartmouth, the Royal Torbay, and the Royal Cornwall at Falmouth. Packs of foxhounds include the Dartmoor, the East Devon, the Mid-Devon and the South Devon, the Dulverton, the East Cornwall and the North Cornwall. Staghounds are the Devon and Somerset and the Tiverton.

GREAT HOUSES AND GARDENS

Among the historic houses in the two counties, the National Trust owns Trerice, Lanhydrock, St Michael's Mount and Cotehele in Cornwall, and Killerton, Saltram, Castle Drogo (designed by Lutyens and the latest great house to be built in England) and Knightshayes in Devon — the last having probably the finest garden in the county. Other notable houses are Mount Edgcumbe near Plymouth, Godolphin near Helston, Hartland Abbey near Bideford and Powderham Castle near Exeter.

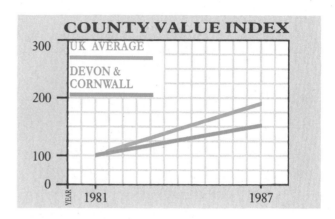

COUNTY VALUE INDEX

UK AVERAGE

DEVON & CORNWALL

(y-axis: 0, 100, 200, 300) (x-axis: 1981, 1987) YEAR

(Far left) **Summer in Padstow** *(Kenneth Scowen).* *(Top left)* **Harled walls of a Cornish house.** *(Middle)* **Well-proportioned Cornish villa.** *(Below)* **Reflected Regency in Devon.**

COMMUNICATIONS

Train connections to Paddington from:

Exeter, fastest travel time	2 hrs 30 mins
off-peak frequency	1 per hour
Plymouth, fastest travel time	3 hrs 30 mins
off-peak frequency	1 per hour
Truro, fastest travel time	4 hrs 20 mins
off-peak frequency	1 every 2 hours

First commuter train to arrive in London at approximately 8.30 a.m.:

from Exeter	6.37 a.m.
from Plymouth	5.40 a.m.

Road distances to central London from:

Exeter (via M5, M4)	174 miles
Plymouth (via A38, M5, M4)	221 miles
Truro (via A39, A30, M5, M4)	257 miles

Airports: Road distances to:

	Newquay	Exeter (miles)	Plymouth
Exeter	78	—	40
Plymouth	45	40	—
Truro	15	85	53

Exeter has scheduled flights to:
Gatwick (1 or 2 per day).
Newquay has scheduled flights to:
Heathrow (1 to 4 per day).
Plymouth has scheduled flights to:
Cork (3 per week).

EAST ANGLIA

CAMBRIDGESHIRE

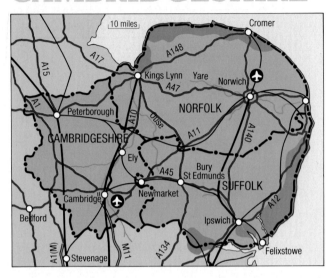

GEOGRAPHY

Cambridgeshire has no sea-coast, but borders on many counties, eight in total. In common with the rest of East Anglia its countryside is flat and low-lying, principally in the north where the fenlands continue from Norfolk. It is therefore not surprising that it has a long history of drainage and land reclamation, dating from Roman times.

The southern half of the county provides a contrast. A chalk plain, it is often called the Southern Uplands, although the maximum height is nowhere above 400 ft. Much of this dry, chalk downland is still devoid of settlement. Agriculture is, and always has been, important, and like Suffolk many of the county's industries, such as milling, brewing and agro-chemicals, are agriculturally based.

The principal rivers are the Cam and the Ouse, and the construction by the Romans of four main roads opened up the county and led to the development of Cambridge where the roads crossed.

Cambridge itself rose to prominence in English and European affairs during the reign of Henry VII. It is not known why the first gathering of scholars came there around 1209, but, by the 13th century, the University was officially recognized. From then until the 15th century 12 colleges were founded and, despite religious controversies, continued to flourish.

MARKET TOWNS

Cambridge is the county town of Cambridgeshire. Other towns are Huntingdon, Ely with its great cathedral, March, Whittlesey, Peterborough with one of the finest Norman cathedral churches in England, Ramsey, St Ives, St Neots and Wisbech.

LEISURE

There is foxhunting with the Fitzwilliam and with the Cambridgeshire; rowing and sailing on the Cam and on a number of other inland waters.

Fishing is available on the Cam and other tributaries of the Great Ouse. There is golf at Ely City, Gog Magog, March, and Thorpe Wood near Peterborough, among other courses.

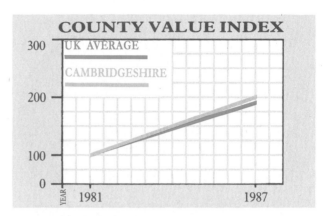

COUNTY VALUE INDEX

UK AVERAGE
CAMBRIDGESHIRE

(Left) **King's College Chapel and Clare College from the Cam** *(Kenneth Scowen).* *(Below left)* **Fine stuccoed villa with tiled roof in Cambridgeshire.** *(Below right)* **Typical 18th-century brick house.**

COMMUNICATIONS

Train connections to Liverpool Street from:

Cambridge, fastest travel time	1 hr 5 mins
off-peak frequency	1 to 2 per hour
Ipswich, fastest travel time	1 hr 5 mins
off-peak frequency	2 per hour
Norwich, fastest travel time	2 hrs 5 mins
off-peak frequency	1 per hour
King's Lynn, fastest travel time	2 hrs 10 mins
off-peak frequency	irregular

First commuter train to arrive in London at approximately 8.30 a.m.:

from Cambridge	7.06 a.m.

Approximate road distances to central London from:

Cambridge (via M11)	54 miles
Ipswich (via A120)	74 miles
Norwich (via A11, M11)	115 miles
King's Lynn (via A10, M11)	97 miles

Airports: Approximate road distances from:

	Heathrow	Gatwick	Stansted
	(miles)		
Cambridge	75	97	25
Ipswich	88	101	49
Norwich	130	145	84
King's Lynn	118	140	70

Regional: Norwich has scheduled flights to:

Aberdeen	1 to 4 per day, not Sat
Amsterdam	1 to 4 per day
Edinburgh	1 to 2 per day, not Sat
Humberside	1 to 5 per day
London Heathrow	1 to 3 per day

GREAT HOUSES AND GARDENS

National Trust properties include Anglesey Abbey with a fine 100-acre garden; Peckover House, Wisbech; the spectacular Wimpole Hall, at Arlington, with a farm that was a world leader when it was designed in 1794.

Other great houses open to the public are Elton Hall; and Docwra's Manor, Shepreth. The East of England agricultural show is held at Peterborough in the latter part of July.

SUFFOLK AND NORFOLK

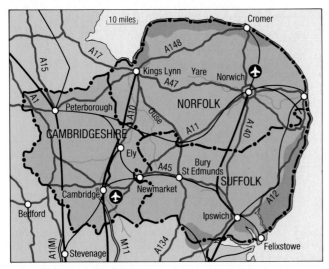

GEOGRAPHY

A characteristic of both these counties is their gently rolling countryside. However, the landscape is more varied and attractive than this might suggest. Suffolk, for instance, is 'Constable country' and, almost entirely surrounded by water, has picturesque coastline, almost all of which is Heritage Coast. A belt of land running parallel alongside the coast is heathland and a designated Area of Outstanding Natural Beauty. In addition, the county possesses part of the Broads, together with pine plantations and mixed woodland, as well as arable farmland.

Suffolk is an agricultural county, the low rainfall and generally flat surface making it particularly suitable for arable crops. The principal industries have agricultural connections, for instance, agricultural machinery and food processing.

Norfolk is usually described as gently rolling, its highest point being 330 ft. above sea level. Though not as varied as its neighbouring county of Suffolk, it does offer some undulating valleys. Norfolk has an island-like quality, with the North Sea on one side and rivers along the others. It also contains many waterways, including the Broads in the north-east. The north-west is fen and marshland; the Wash gives it a tide-washed, sand-and-mud wilderness providing a rich habitat for bird life. Much of the coastline is reclaimed from the sea.

The central and southern part of Norfolk comprises pasture and fertile farmland, with the Breckland heathland in the south-west and the Thetford forest, one of England's largest. Norfolk is one of the driest counties, with less than 30 inches of rainfall annually. The main rivers are the Ouse in the north-west, the Wissey and the Yare in the east, and the Waveney running into the North Sea at Great Yarmouth.

In Saxon times Suffolk and Norfolk were wealthy. Domesday showed Norfolk to be the most populous part of England, and Suffolk, almost as densely populated, had more

Suffolk landscape near Lavenham *(Kenneth Scowen).* *(Below right)* **A former Suffolk rectory.** *(Far right)* **A spacious twin-gabled brick house in Norfolk.**

towns with markets than any other county. That early wealth was based on agriculture and the ports. Suffolk had an established woollen trade in the later Middle Ages, and Norfolk an important fishing industry.

MARKET TOWNS

Administratively, Suffolk is divided into East and West, the western centre being Bury St Edmunds and the eastern Ipswich. Other towns are Lowestoft, Woodbridge, Sudbury, Halesworth, Aldeburgh, Felixstowe, Hadleigh, Stowmarket, Southwold, Leiston, Saxmundham and Beccles.

Norwich is the county town of Norfolk. Great Yarmouth on the east coast is a large holiday resort. Other towns are Thetford, Kings Lynn, Fakenham, Downham Market, Wymondham, North Walsham, Cromer, Diss, East Dereham, Holt, Sheringham, Hunstanton and Swaffham.

SUFFOLK AND NORFOLK

LEISURE

Foxhunting is with the West Norfolk, the Suffolk and the Essex and Suffolk. East Anglia is renowned for its pheasant shooting. Fishing is abundant in many waters, notably the Great Ouse and its tributaries, the Yare, the Waveney and the Bure. There are many sailing centres, and the Broads offer their own unique sailing facilities. The Broads Authority has now been constituted with a status similar to that of a National Park. Many distinguished golf courses include the Royal West Norfolk at Brancaster, Royal Norwich and Royal Cromer.

Newmarket justly claims to be the capital of the horse-racing world. In 1987 it modernised its facilities with a £4 million grandstand redevelopment on the historic Rowley Mile. Newmarket already offers a 29-day racing year, with spring and autumn meetings on the Rowley Mile and summer meetings on the July course, and is planning further expansion. There is also flat racing at Yarmouth and National Hunt racing at Fakenham.

GREAT HOUSES AND GARDENS

National Trust properties include Blickling Hall, Norwich; Felbrigg Hall, Norwich; Oxburgh Hall, near King's Lynn; and Melford Hall, near Sudbury. The Trust also owns areas of coast at Blakeney Point and elsewhere. Other house open to the public include Houghton Hall, near King's Lynn; Oakleigh House, Swaffham; Sandringham House (not open when the Queen or other members of the Royal Family are in residence); Walsingham Abbey; and Euston Hall, Thetford.

The principal agricultural show is the East of England, held at Peterborough in the latter part of July.

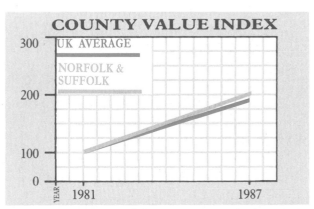

COUNTY VALUE INDEX

(graph showing lines for UK AVERAGE and NORFOLK & SUFFOLK, Y-axis 0 to 300, X-axis YEAR 1981 to 1987)

(Top left) **The Market Square in Woodbridge, Suffolk** *(Kenneth Scowen).* *(Left)* **View in Elm Hill, Norwich** *(Kenneth Scowen).* *(Below left)* **A fine Norfolk house with stepped gables.** *(Below right)* **Mellowed brick and typical Suffolk chimneys.**

COMMUNICATIONS

Train connections to Liverpool Street from:

Cambridge, fastest travel time	1 hr 5 mins
off-peak frequency	1 to 2 per hour
Ipswich, fastest travel time	1 hr 5 mins
off-peak frequency	2 per hour
Norwich, fastest travel time	2 hrs 5 mins
off-peak frequency	1 per hour
King's Lynn, fastest travel time	2 hrs 10 mins
off-peak frequency	irregular

First commuter train to arrive in London at approximately 8.30 a.m.:

from Ipswich	7.05 a.m.
from Norwich	5.58 a.m.
from King's Lynn	6.15 a.m.

Approximate road distances to central London from:

Cambridge (via M11)	54 miles
Ipswich (via A120)	74 miles
Norwich (via A11, M11)	115 miles
King's Lynn (via A10, M11)	97 miles

Airports: Approximate road distances from:

	Heathrow	Gatwick	Stanstead
		(miles)	
Cambridge	75	97	25
Ipswich	88	101	49
Norwich	130	145	84
King's Lynn	118	140	70

Regional: Norwich has scheduled flights to:

Aberdeen	1 to 4 per day, not Sat.
Amsterdam	1 to 4 per day
Edinburgh	1 to 2 per day, not Sat.
Humberside	1 to 5 per day
London Heathrow	1 to 3 per day

NORTHAMPTONSHIRE & BEDFORDSHIRE

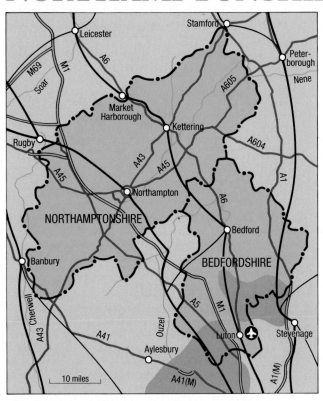

MARKET TOWNS

Bedford is the county town of Bedfordshire. Other towns are Luton, Ampthill, Biggleswade, Leighton Buzzard and Dunstable.

In Northamptonshire, Northampton is the county town. Other towns are Wellingborough, Kettering, Rushden, Corby and Daventry.

LEISURE

Northamptonshire is one of the primary foxhunting counties, and the Pytchley ranks with the great Leicestershire packs, part of its country lying in that county. Other hunts are the Woodland Pytchley, the Oakley (partly in Bedfordshire) and the Grafton.

There is National Hunt racing at Towcester from November to May. Burghley is the site of one of the most celebrated three-day events. Fishing waters include the Tove and the Ouse. Reservoirs and lakes include Cransley Reservoir at Kettering and Fawsley Park Lakes at Daventry.

GEOGRAPHY

Both of these counties are fairly small and possess little in the way of spectacular scenery. However, they do have landscapes that are uniform and pleasant, with Northamptonshire thrusting to a height of 804 ft. in the west and Bedfordshire claiming part of an Area of Outstanding Natural Beauty in its south-eastern corner. This is part of a chalk escarpment. In the north east there lies the attractive Ouse valley. Both counties are within commuting distance of London, although certainly Northamptonshire is far enough away to have escaped major development.

At the advent of the Industrial Revolution, Bedfordshire was still a farming county. However, the coming of the railways heralded the development of industry within the county, principally engineering. Northamptonshire had an important position under the Romans, with numerous lines of communication, including Watling Street, and a number of forts and villas.

The 16th-century architecture of Northamptonshire is regarded as some of the most important in England for that period. It was from this time onwards that a succession of country houses were built up until the 18th century. Bedfordshire has little domestic architecture dating from before the 17th century. However, it does possess fine country houses of subsequent periods.

Golf courses include South Bedfordshire, at Luton; Steventon Park at Daventry, Stockwood Park at Luton, and Wellingborough.

GREAT HOUSES AND GARDENS

National Trust properties in Northamptonshire include Canons Ashby House, near Daventry, and Lyveden New Field, near Oundle. Private houses and gardens open to the public in Bedfordshire include Luton Hoo, Luton; the Swin Garden near Biggleswade; Woburn Abbey, home of the Dukes of Bedford for over three centuries; and Wrest Park House and Gardens at Silsoe.

In Northamptonshire are Althorp, seat of the Earl Spencer and ancestral home of the Princess of Wales; Boughton House, Kettering, where the Duke of Buccleuch is pioneering new techniques in the opening of great estates to the public; Burghley House, Stamford, claimed to be the finest example of late Elizabethan architecture in England and home of the Cecils for 400 years; Castle Ashby near Northampton; Deene Park near Corby, home of the

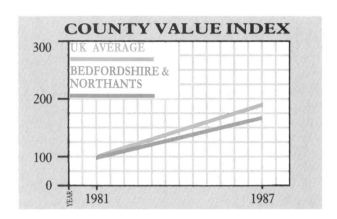

Brudenell family since 1514; Rockingham Castle near Corby; and Sulgrave Manor, home of George Washington's ancestors.

Public schools include Oundle.

(Far left) **In the village of Rockingham, Northamptonshire** *(Kenneth Scowen).* *(Left)* **A fine Bedfordshire stone house with tiled roof.** *(Below left)* **Mellowed stone, gable and finials in Northamptonshire.**

COMMUNICATIONS

 Train connections to Euston or King's Cross from:

Northampton, fastest travel time	56 mins
off-peak frequency	1 per hr
Bedford, fastest travel time	47 mins
off-peak frequency	3 per hr
Kettering, fastest travel time	52 mins
off-peak frequency	1 per hr

First commuter train to arrive in London at approximately 8.30 a.m.:

from Northampton	7.20 a.m.
from Bedford	7.37 a.m.
from Kettering	7.35 a.m.

 Approximate road distances to central London from:

Northampton, (via M10)	58 miles
Bedford (via A6, M1)	40 miles
Kettering (via A43, M1)	72 miles

 Airports: Approximate road distance from:

	Luton	Heathrow	Gatwick
		(miles)	
Northampton	33	74	100
Bedford	19	58	85
Kettering	47	89	116

LINCOLNSHIRE

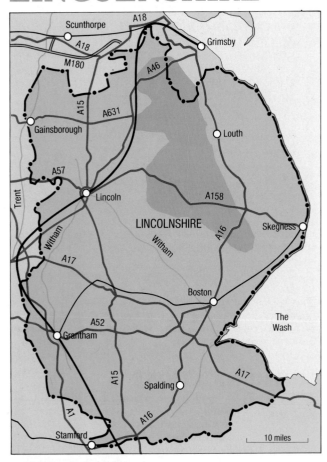

GEOGRAPHY

Lincolnshire's landscape is of two strongly contrasting kinds. One is level, wide and expansive, the other hilly and rolling. It is the southern parts of Lincolnshire that contain the wide-open and level countryside. Part of the Fens is named 'Holland', in reference to its flat land and the fields of bulbs and flowers that cover it. The Fenland itself is not all adjoining the sea, but is drained inland countryside that, as well as producing flowers, is rich cornland.

In the south-east is the flat coastal region where Skegness and other resorts are located. Here are the marshland and low-lying pastureland, interlaced with dykes and meres, stretching along the sea coast between the Wash and the Humber. The Wash itself is an unique area. A vast stretch of flat, tide-washed sand and mud, surrounded by sea-walls, it is inhabited by a great variety of birdlife.

As one travels west and north, the land of Lincolnshire folds up into undulating valleys which are clothed in trees and other vegetation. In the north-east, and inland slightly, are the Lincolnshire Wolds, an Area of Outstanding Natural Beauty. These chalk hills appear high in contrast to the flatlands of the south, although they never reach over 500 ft. To the north is another, adjoining, upland area, composed of limestone scarp. Also to be found here is the Lincoln Heath. Lincolnshire is one of the country's driest counties.

Until 1974, the county was divided into three units, Lindsey, Kesteven and Holland. With the local government re-organisation of 1974, the strip of land was lost to Humberside. This was an area that had been the county's main industrial region and had contained the largest town, Grimsby. It was the Romans who first fortified the area against the sea and began to drain the Fens. They also appeared to favour the area, using the county as a settlement for retired legionnaires. When the Romans left the county, it formed part of Mercia, until the Danish invasion when it became part of Danelaw.

Under Norman rule the prosperity of the county was such that Lincoln almost outdid London in population-growth and trade. This prosperity did not last, first declining in the 14th century. The 18th century saw some improvement, as new agricultural techniques increased production and the new industrial regions of the North and Midlands created demand.

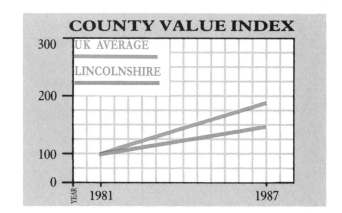

COUNTY VALUE INDEX

(Far left) **Classical Lincolnshire house.** *(Left)* **The Norman façade of Lincoln Cathedral** *(Kenneth Scowen).*

MARKET TOWNS

Lincoln is the county town, famous for its historic cathedral. Other towns are Grantham, Spalding, Louth, Boston, Gainsborough, Sleaford and Bourne.

LEISURE

Foxhunting flourishes in the county. Packs include the Brocklesby, the Burton, and the Blankney. There is sailing from a number of harbours along the coast. Fishing rivers include the Witham and the Welland. There is golf at Blankney, Boston, Burghley Park, Lincoln, Louth, Luffenham Heath and Sandilands (at Sutton-on-Sea).

GREAT HOUSES AND GARDENS

National Trust properties include Belton House at Grantham, Grantham House, Gunby Hall near Spilsby and Tattershall Castle. Other properties open to the public include Doddington Hall; Grimsthorpe Castle; Harrington Hall; and the Old Hall at Gainsborough.

Lincolnshire Agricultural Show is held at Grange de Lings, Lincoln, in the latter part of June.

COMMUNICATIONS

Train connections to King's Cross from:

Lincoln, fastest travel time	1 hr 58 mins
off-peak frequency	1 per 2 hrs
Skegness, fastest travel time	3 hrs 15 mins
off-peak frequency	1 per 2 hrs
Grantham, fastest travel time	1 hr 8 mins
off-peak frequency	1 per hr

First commuter train to arrive in London at approximately 8.30 a.m.:

from Lincoln	6.32 a.m.
from Grantham	7.18 a.m.

Approximate road distances to central London from:

Lincoln (via A15, A1(M))	131 miles
Skegness (via A1(M))	136 miles
Grantham (via A1, A1(M))	106 miles

Regional airports: Approximate road distance from:

	Leeds	Manchester
	(miles)	
Lincoln	68	82
Skegness	108	122
Grantham	75	96

Leeds airport has scheduled flight to:
Heathrow, 2 to 6 per day
Gatwick, 1 to 3 per day

Manchester airport has 59 international departures and scheduled flights to:
Heathrow, 7 to 10 per day
Gatwick, 2 to 5 per day

NOTTINGHAMSHIRE, DERBYSHIRE AND

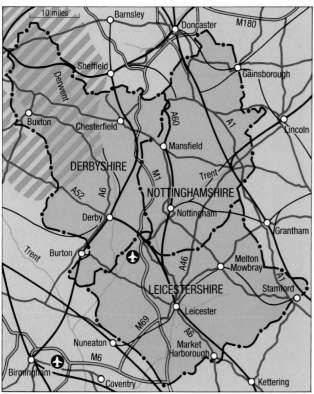

GEOGRAPHY

Leicestershire is often considered to be the heart of England, although it is one of the least visited of its counties. It has a considerable range and variety of bedrocks. In the north lies ancient, hard basement rock which is common also to much of Wales and the Pennines. To the south is the softer strata of east and south England. The county is roughly divided east-west by the Soar Valley. In the East is the higher land of the marlestone escarpment, where much of the countryside is over 600 ft.

To the north-east is the Vale of Belvoir, fertile countryside — indeed this eastern half of the county is primarily agricultural. In the north-west lies Charnwood Forest, not now a forest, but in the past a hunting park.

Derbyshire too can be divided, but in this case between north and south. The north-west contains the Derbyshire Peak District, Britain's oldest National Park. The county also boasts Britain's oldest Country Park. The Peak District is in fact part of the Southern Pennines and peat moorland, 2,000 ft. high. Compared to the southern part of the county, this region receives twice the volume of rainfall and, on average, a 10 °F lower temperature.

The south-east is more populated than the other areas and has most of the county's industry. However, the more open and higher land to the north and west has become an

important tourist area. The Derwent is the most significant river; there are also the Trent, Wye and Dove.

In contrast to Derbyshire, Nottinghamshire has little spectacular scenery. The gently rolling countryside gives way to little high land, and the county has been described as one where everything occurs on a small scale. The west has the oldest rock, and has important coal mines. Sherwood Forest lies to the north-east, although a belt of land running north-south still retains some tracts of the once extensive forest. In the forest is part of the Leicestershire Wolds. The river Trent runs north-east and south-west.

MARKET TOWNS

Leicestershire's principal market towns are Melton Mowbray, Market Harborough, Oakham, Hinckley, Coalville, Ashby de la Zouch, Loughborough, Lutterworth and Uppingham.

In Derbyshire, they are Chesterfield, Bakewell (capital of the Peak District), Ashbourne, Matlock, Derby, Alfreton, Ikeston, Belper, Swadlincote, Heanor, Buxton, Glossop and New Mills. There is no typical Derbyshire village, because of the wide variety of landscape and building material within the county.

The Nottinghamshire towns include Mansfield, Kirkby-in-Ashfield, Newark-on-Trent, Beeston, and East Retford.

LEISURE

Leicestershire is the most celebrated foxhunting county in England, and therefore in the world. The historic packs are the Quorn, the Belvoir, the Fernie and the Atherstone.

Nottinghamshire has the South Notts and the Grove and Rufford. In Derbyshire are the Barlow and part of the

LEICESTERSHIRE

Meynell country. Of course none of these hunting countries fits precisely within county boundaries, because they have been drawn up for sporting, not administrative reasons. There is both flat and National Hunt racing at Nottingham and Leicester and racing under N. H. rules at Southwell.

Golf courses include Allestree Park, Derby; Ashbourne, Derbyshire; Derby; Erewash Valley, Derbyshire; Birstall, Leicester; Bulwell Forest, Nottingham; Glen Gorse, Leicester; Newark, Nottinghamshire; Rothley Park, Leicester; and Sherwood Forest, Nottinghamshire.

Fishing rivers include the Trent and the Welland and their tributaries. Inland waters include Rutland Water.

At Holme Pierrepont, just outside Nottingham, is the National Watersports Centre, with a six-lane Olympic-standard rowing course, created out of a chain of quarries.

An outstanding cricket team in the second half of the 19th century, Nottinghamshire have had less success in the 20th despite being the breeding ground of some fine cricketers, including the fast bowlers Larwood and Voce. The county ground, Trent Bridge, is also a Test Match venue.

Derbyshire have never been a force in county cricket, but have produced a succession of England-class fast-medium bowlers and a very fine wicketkeeper in Bob Taylor. Derby, Chesterfield and Buxton are the main county grounds. The hunting county of Leicestershire (whose crest is a running fox) have won the county cricket championship on only one occasion (in 1975).

GREAT HOUSES AND GARDENS

National Trust properties in Nottinghamshire include Clumber Park, with 3,800 acres of park and farmland. In

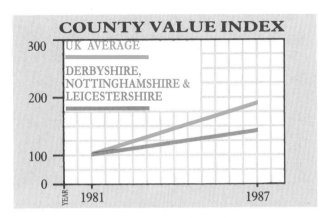

COUNTY VALUE INDEX

Derbyshire are the Calke Abbey estate of 2,172 acres, as well as part of Dovedale and the moorland of Kinder Scout.

Great houses in private hands, open to the public, include Holme Pierrepont Hall and Newstead Abbey in Nottinghamshire; Chatsworth, Haddon Hall, Hardwich Hall, Kedleston Hall and Melbourne Hall in Derbyshire; Belvoir Castle, and Oakham Castle, Leicestershire.

(Left) **A corner by the church in Oakham, Leicestershire** *(Kenneth Scowen).* *(Right)* **Typical Derbyshire stone house.**

COMMUNICATIONS

Train connections to St Pancras from:

Chesterfield, fastest travel time	2 hrs 7 mins
off-peak frequency	1 per hour
Nottingham, fastest travel time	1 hr 50 mins
off-peak frequency	1 per hour
Leicester, fastest travel time	1 hr 17 mins
off-peak frequency	2 per hour

First commuter train to arrive in London at approximately 8.30 a.m.:

from Nottingham	6.00 a.m.
from Leicester	7.09 a.m.

Approximate road distances to central London from:

Chesterfield (via A617, M1)	152 miles
Nottingham (via M1)	128 miles
Leicester (via M1)	105 miles

Airports: Near to Birmingham, which has around 27 international departures and scheduled flights to:
Heathrow, 1 to 6 per day
Gatwick, 1 to 3 per day

Also near to Manchester, which has 59 international departures and scheduled flights to:
Heathrow, 7 to 9 per day
Gatwick 2 to 7 per day

WEST MIDLANDS

WARWICKSHIRE

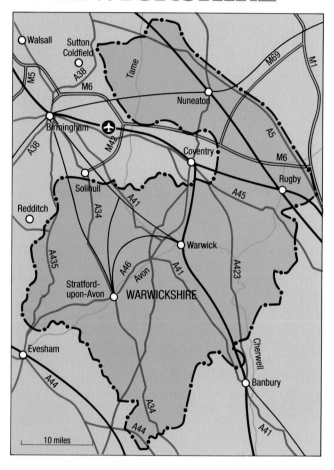

A fine classical house in Warwickshire. *(Below)* Well-proportioned brick house with steep pitched roof. *(Right)* Warwick Castle above the Avon *(Kenneth Scowen)*.

GEOGRAPHY

Warwickshire is the heart of England. There are three places that claim the title of being the exact centre of the country, the cross at Meriden, High Cross on Watling Street, and an oak tree near Lillington. It is a populous county, mainly due to Birmingham and Coventry in the north.

However, the urban sprawl has not taken over the county, and much of it remains engaged in prosperous farming and market gardening. The landscape is primarily one of green fields and isolated villages.

There are two main types of countryside: the woodlands north of the Arden and the more open landscape south of the river. The Forest of Arden was never a continuous forest, but a district of dense wood interspersed with shrubland. There has always been some mystery about it, and it is probably one of the most romantic forests in British folklore, due to its associations with the centre of the English world.

In the past the county was called 'leafy Warwickshire'. The southern end of the county contains part of the Cotswolds. This is the main agricultural area and has some of

WARWICKSHIRE

the highest land, rising to 850 ft. along the south-east border with Oxfordshire. It is rich arable land, with undulating hills, woodland, leafy lanes bordered by thriving hedgerows and quiet streams.

MARKET TOWNS

The town of Warwick is thought to have been founded around the 6th or early 7th century, and the shire surrounding it during the 10th. Warwick Castle was built in 1068 by William the Conqueror. It was involved in numerous battles, including Edgehill. Stratford-upon-Avon has long thrived, and has developed an important tourist trade, as the birthplace of Shakespeare and the site of the Royal Shakespeare Theatre. Other towns are Rugby, Kenilworth, Southam and Royal Leamington Spa. The principal public school in the county is Rugby.

LEISURE

There is foxhunting with the Warwickshire, and the Croome and West Warwickshire. Meets of the North Cotswold, Grafton, Heythrop and Bicester can also be reached. The presence of the National Equestrian Centre at Stoneleigh, with the headquarters of the British Horse Society and other horse organisations, is one reason why the county is exceptionally well provided with equestrian events.

There is flat racing at Warwick and National Hunt racing at Stratford-upon-Avon. The county cricket ground is at Edgbaston.

Principal fishing rivers are the Avon and tributaries. The Tame, in the care of the Severn-Trent Water Authority, has recovered after long years of pollution. Golf courses include Kenilworth, Leamington and County and many courses round Birmingham and Coventry.

(Left) **Royal Shakespeare Theatre, Stratford-upon-Avon** (Kenneth Scowen). **Mill Street, Warwick** (Kenneth Scowen). (Below) **An enlarged classical house in Warwickshire.**

The principal agricultural show is, of course, the Royal Show at Stoneleigh, sited there primarily because of its central position and accessibility.

GREAT HOUSES AND GARDENS

National Trust properties include the medieval manor of Baddesley Clinton; the 16th-century house at Charlecote with its park said to have been poached by Shakespeare and which was later landscaped by Capability Brown; Coughton Court, associated with the Gunpowder Plot; Packwood House near Solihull, and Upton House at Edgehill.

Other important houses open to the public are Stoneleigh Abbey, Ragley Hall near Alcester, Warwick Castle, Arbury Hall near Nuneaton, and Kenilworth Castle, in the care of English Heritage.

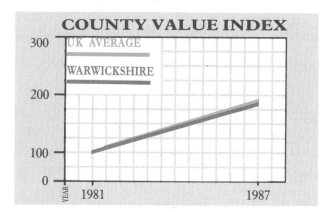

COUNTY VALUE INDEX

UK AVERAGE

WARWICKSHIRE

300

200

100

0

YEAR   1981   1987

COMMUNICATIONS

Train connections to Euston or Paddington from:
Warwick, fastest travel time	2 hrs
off-peak frequency	1 per hr
Stratford-upon-Avon, fastest travel time	
	1 hr 50 mins
off-peak frequency	1 per 2 hrs
Coventry, fastest travel time	2 hrs
off-peak frequency	2 per hr

First commuter train to arrive in London at approximately 8.30 a.m.:
from Coventry   7.10 a.m.

Approximate road distances to central London from:
Warwick (via A45, M1)	90 miles
Stratford-upon-Avon (via A34, A40, M1)	89 miles
Coventry (via M6, M1)	92 miles

Airports: Near to Birmingham which has 27 international departures and scheduled flights to:
Heathrow, 1 to 6 per day
Gatwick, 1 to 3 per day

SHROPSHIRE

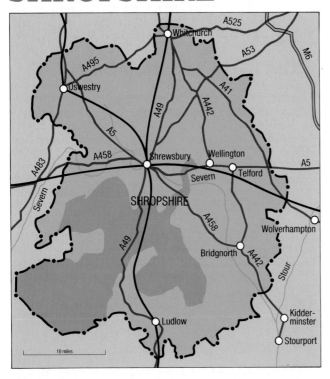

GEOGRAPHY

Shropshire has the smallest population of any English county excepting Northumberland. The lack of bridges spanning the Severn has given the region some isolation, resulting in its being remarkably unspoilt.

The extreme north-west of the county merges with part of the Welsh uplands, giving a landscape of small, crowded hills. However, the majority of this northern area is composed of an undulating plain formed by glacial drifts, and is rich arable and dairy-farming land. In the north-east is the Shropshire coalfield.

The southern half of Shropshire is an area of upland providing constrasting scenery. A series of hill ranges, including Wenlock Edge and the Stretton Hills, is designated an Area of Outstanding Natural Beauty. The central and western ranges are fingers of the Welsh mountains reaching into England. Barren and isolated, these hills almost qualify as mountains. Mainly hill farming country, the area is interspersed with scattered hamlets and villages, with fertile valleys lying between them. The eastern slopes are of gentler shape. These hills provide good walking country and have been preserved from urban development by their relative isolation.

Running north-west to south-east is the Severn, Britain's longest river. Flowing from the Welsh mountains, it divides the county roughly in half. The stately Severn is one of Shropshire's chief features. Its functions have included giving

power to industry, providing sport for anglers and impeding the advance of invaders.

The county's border position is reflected in the landscape, the most obvious reminder of the Saxon inhabitants being Offa's Dyke, the first serious attempt to settle the Welsh Border. There are many hill-top forts and a number of Norman castles.

Shropshire is a county of innumerable tiny hamlets. There are a number of reasons for this: the area is not under commuter pressure; many potential villages were lost at the time of the Enclosures, and later with the decline of lead mining and quarrying.. Though the villages are small, an important element in the Shropshire landscape is the large houses and estates. It was during the 17th and 18th centuries that the most ambitious houses were built. Black-and-white timber-framed houses are common.

MARKET TOWNS

Shrewsbury is the county town. Other towns are Bishops Castle, Bridgnorth, Church Stretton, Ellesmere, Ludlow, Market Drayton, Telford, Whitchurch, Oswestry, Shifnal,

Late Georgian house in Shropshire. *(Top right)* **View of Wenlock Edge from the Long Mynd** *(Kenneth Scowen).* *(Below, right)* **Broad Gate, Ludlow** *(Kenneth Scowen).*

Wellington and Newport. Most of the towns date to Saxon or Roman times and have a range of medieval, Georgian and Victorian architecture. The Ellesmere area is called the Shropshire Lake District.

LEISURE

There is foxhunting with the North Shropshire, the South Shropshire, the Ludlow and the United. Ludlow offers racing under National Hunt rules from September to May. There is fishing on the Severn and its many tributaries as well as on a number of Shropshire lakes. Golf courses include Oswestry, Church Stretton, Bridgnorth and Hill Valley, Whitchurch.

GREAT HOUSES AND GARDENS

National Trust houses in Shropshire include Attingham Park, Shrewsbury, with its park landscaped by Humphry Repton; Benthall Hall, Broseley; Dudmaston and Morville Hall, near Bridgnorth and Wilderhope Manor, Much Wenlock, now a YHA hostel. Countryside is the care of the Trust includes the Long Mynd.

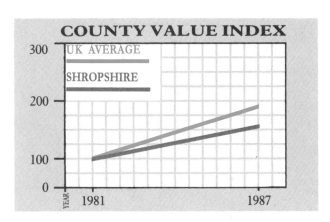

English Heritage has Boscobel House, Shifnal, and Wenlock Priory.

Other notable properties open to the public include Mawley Hall, Cleobury Mortimer; Hodnet Hall Gardens, Market Drayton; and Tyn-y-Rhos Hall, near Oswestry, with Welsh royal connections.

The county's most celebrated school is, of course, Shrewsbury.

The Shropshire and West Midlands Agricultural Show is held towards the end of May at Shrewsbury.

COMMUNICATIONS

Train connections to Euston or Paddington from:
Shrewsbury, fastest travel time — 2 hrs 55 mins
   off-peak frequency — 1 per hr
Ludlow, fastest travel time — 3 hrs 15 mins
   off-peak frequency — 1 per 2 hrs
Whitchurch, fastest travel time — 2 hrs 45 mins
   off-peak frequency — 1 per hr
Also, via Stafford, fastest travel time 1 hr 40 mins
   off-peak frequency — 1 per hr

First commuter train to arrive in London at approximately 8.30 a.m.:
from Shrewsbury — 6.20 a.m.

Approximate road distances to central London from:
Shrewsbury (via M54, M6, M1) — 162 miles
Ludlow (via A44, M5) — 135 miles
Whitchurch (via A41, M6, M1) — 182 miles

Airports: Close to Birmingham which has 27 international departures and scheduled flights to:
   Heathrow, 1 to 6 per day
   Gatwick, 1 to 3 per day
Close to Manchester which has 59 international departures and scheduled flights to:
   Heathrow, 7 to 9 per day
   Gatwick, 2 to 7 per day

CHESHIRE AND STAFFORDSHIRE

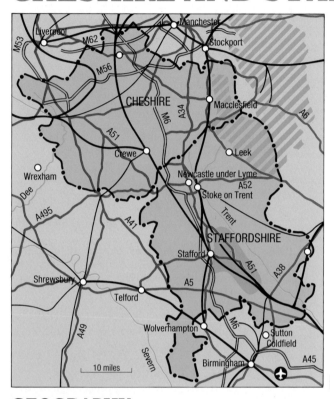

GEOGRAPHY

Both counties have a varied physical character. Staffordshire, although compact, is not a natural self-contained area. The southern Black Country is part of the West Midland plateau, while, in the south-west lie the fertile Tame and Trent valleys. The Trent is the county's main river, and its valley is a lush corridor, running east-west. Northwards, the central area of the county is rich farmland, interspersed with characteristic red-brick farmhouses. In the northern portion, there is further variation in the landscape. Here are the heights of the south-western Pennines known as the Staffordshire Moorlands, and an extension of the Peak District.

The rock of the upland areas, both those of the north and the south, is a combination of limestone, sandstone and coal. It was the coal, mined in both regions, that formed the basis for industrial development, and resulted in the county's two major conurbations. The Potteries, round Stoke-on-Trent, have long been the centre of the ceramics industry. Staffordshire is reputed to be the county furthest from the sea, but the claim is disputed with Warwickshire.

Cheshire, north-west of Staffordshire, does not possess such diversity in its landscape. The greater part of the county is a large plain, with the Wirral peninsula in the north. Meadows and woodland are the major constituents. However, there is some variety, with the isolated hill ranges of Alderley Edge and the Pack-Forton Hills. The east

presents a sudden change, with the high, bleak moors that are part of the Peak District National Park, whose highest point reaches almost 2,000 ft. A mainly agricultural county, the other industries are salt, chemicals and ship-building. It has long been a renowned cheese-producing region.

MARKET TOWNS

In Staffordshire the county town is Stafford. Other towns include Lichfield, Cannock, Cheadle, Stone, Stoke, Leek, Uttoxeter, Burton on Trent and Rugeley.

In Cheshire, Chester is the county town, of Roman origins. Other towns include Macclesfield, Nantwich, Ellesmere Port, the railway centre of Crewe and Sandbach.

A gracious house with fine ironwork in a mature setting. *(Below)* **On the Staffordshire border near Alstonfield** *(Kenneth Scowen).*

LEISURE

Foxhunting is with the Cheshire, the Cheshire Forest, the North Staffordshire, the Meynell and South Staffordshire, the Albrighton and the Albrighton Woodland. There is flat racing at Chester and National Hunt racing at Uttoxeter.

Fishing comes partly under the North-West Water Authority and partly under the Severn-Trent Water Authority. The rivers include Izaak Walton's Dove, the Derwent and its tributaries, and the Tame and the Dee.

Golf courses include Alderley Edge, Astbury, Beau Desert near Cannock, Brocton Hall, Drayton Park, Ingestre, Stafford Castle and Trentham Park.

In Milldale, Staffordshire *(Kenneth Scowen). (Below)* The Chester Rows *(Kenneth Scowen).*

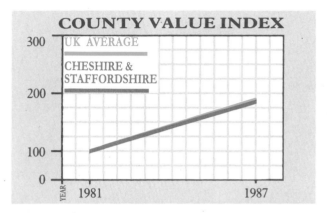

COUNTY VALUE INDEX

GREAT HOUSES AND GARDENS

National Trust properties in Cheshire include Dunham Massey Hall, near Altrincham; Tatton Park, Knutsford; and Little Moreton Hall, one of the finest half-timbered moated manor houses. Properties in Staffordshire include Ilam Hall and Country Park near Ashbourne; Moseley Old Hall near Wolverhampton; and Shugborough, near Stafford.

Other properties open to the public include, in Cheshire: Cholmondeley Castle Gardens, Malpas; Capesthorne near Macclesfield (home of the Bromley-Davenport family); Beeston Castle (English Heritage) Peover Hall, Knutsford; and Vale Royal Abbey, at Whitegate. In Staffordshire are Eccleshell Castle, Stafford, and Hench Hall, near Lichfield.

COMMUNICATIONS

Train connections to Euston from:

Chester, fastest travel time	2 hrs 35 mins
off-peak frequency	irregular
Stafford, fastest travel time	1 hr 40 mins
off-peak frequency	1 per hr
Stoke on Trent, fastest travel time	1 hr 50 mins
off-peak frequency	1 per hr

First commuter train to arrive in London at approximately 8.30 a.m.:

from Stoke	7.04 a.m.

Approximate road distances to central London from:

Chester (via A51, (M6))	184 miles
Stafford (via M6)	129 miles
Stoke on Trent (via M6)	156 miles

Airports: Close to Manchester which has about 59 international departures and scheduled flights to London:

Heathrow, 7 to 10 per day
Gatwick, 2 to 5 per day

Also nearby is Liverpool Airport, which has scheduled flights to London:

Heathrow, 3 to 5 per day

THE NORTH

YORKSHIRE AND HUMBERSIDE

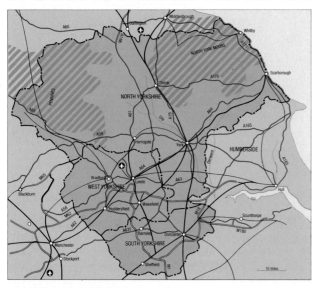

GEOGRAPHY

England's largest county, Yorkshire, can be roughly divided into two halves. The northern half is mostly agricultural, the southern, industrial. This is a very rough generalisation, as the county contains wide variety and contrasting scenery. The industrial cities of Leeds, Bradford and Huddersfield developed around the coalfields of the south of the county. The plain of Yorkshire lies centrally, and is pastoral in character, consisting of the Vale of York, Pickering and Howden. However, the most characteristic feature of this area is the uplands. The Pennine hills, the backbone of England, run down the western length of the county. Some of the highest of the peaks are here, for example, Ingleborough and Whernside, with their fine limestone scenery. Steeper in the west, the Pennines were scoured during the Ice Age, and have been left with numerous small lakes and tarns. These western fells form the Yorkshire Dales.

The second area is the North Yorkshire Moors. Wild, windswept moorland, with hidden valleys, provides good walking country. The third contrasting landscape, in the northern part of Yorkshire, is its coastline, with dramatic cliffs and pleasant villages. Towns like Scarborough and Filey have become holiday resorts, and the picturesque fishing villages of Whitby and Robin Hood's Bay are great tourist attractions.

The Derwent is the principal river of the county, flowing from the Howardian Hills and across the Vale of York. The Derwent valley is surrounded by an arcadian landscape of gentle countryside. Its unpolluted waters provide a home for a great variety of wildlife, as well as excellent sport for anglers. The county has a fairly cold climate, particularly upon the higher land.

The pattern of land division within Yorkshire — the three Ridings, North, East and West, are a Scandinavian legacy. The term 'Riding' is derived from the old Norse meaning 'third'.

York has been a city of political and religious eminence throughout history from Viking times onward, and the county was involved in the Wars of the Roses and the Civil War. Industrialisation came early to the county with the discovery and exploitation of coal, lead and other metallic ores.

Humberside is a small county whose principal treasure is a 50-mile stretch of unspoilt coastline. The region surrounding Flamborough Head is a designated Heritage Coast. Almost all of the area is in agriculture, but the county also possesses timber, agricultural processing plants and chemical companies. The east coast is an unspoilt part of Humberside that includes the resorts of Bridlington, Hornsea and Cleethorpes. The southern border was once formed by the Humber estuary, but since the local government reorganisation in 1974, a belt of land stretching to Grimsby has been incorporated from Lincolnshire. The main river is the Derwent, which forms the western boundary.

MARKET TOWNS

There are several large cities in or bordering on to Yorshire, notably York, Sheffield and Doncaster. Market towns include Ripon, Knaresborough, Haworth, Leyburn, Richmond, Guisborough, Pickering, Harrogate, Selby, Thirsk, Scarborough, Bridlington, Filey, Malton, Pickering, Whitby, Northallerton, Settle and Skipton.

In Humberside, Hull is the principal city, followed by Grimsby. Also there are Beverley, Market Weighton, Pocklington, Driffield and Bridlington.

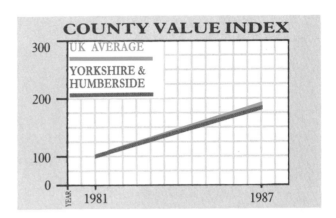

(Far.left) **Well-proportioned stone house with shallow pitched roofs.** (Left) **The Shambles in York** (Kenneth Scowen).

LEISURE

Yorkshire is one of the greatest of sporting counties. Renowned packs of hounds include the Bedale, the Cleveland, the Middleton, the York and Ainsty (North), the York and Ainsty (South), the Zetland (partly in Durham), the Bramham Moor, the Holderness and the Badsworth — a roll-call difficult to surpass.

It is not surprising that the county is also known for its horse-breeding, among the celebrated products being the Cleveland Bay.

The exceptionally large number of racecourses is also indicative of the horse's role. There is flat racing at Catterick, Redcar, Thirsk, Ripon, York, Beverley and Pontefract; flat racing and NH racing at Catterick and Doncaster; and NH racing at Wetherby.

The Yorkshire Water Authority controls the fishing in a wide network of rivers and other inland waters; the Fisheries Manager is at Rivers Division, YWA, 21 Park Square South, Leeds LS1 2QG.

Among golf courses are the Alwoodley near Leeds; the Garforth; the Hallamshire, near Sheffield; the Moor Allerton; the Sandmoor, near Leeds, and the Gantoy, near Scarborough, where Harry Vardon was professional in the 1890s.

Yorkshire's record in county cricket is formidable: champion county in 1893, '96, '98, 1900, 1901, 1902, just to pick a single short period; and again in 1959, '60, '62, '63, '66, '67 and '68, to take a more recent short spell. The county ground is at Headingley.

GREAT HOUSES AND GARDENS

National Trust properties in Yorkshire include Nostell Priory, Wakefield; Fountains Abbey and Studley Royal, Ripon; and Beningbrough Hall near York. The long list of other great houses open to the public includes Castle Howard, York; Hoveningham Hall, north of York; Newburgh Priory, Coxwold; Skipton Castle; Bramham Park; Wetherby; Harewood House, Leeds, Temple Newsam House, Leeds. In Humberside are Normanby Hall, Scunthorpe; Burton Constable, near Hull; and Carlton Towers, near Goole.

Famous schools include Ampleforth.

The Great Yorkshire Show is held at Harrogate in the middle of July.

COMMUNICATIONS

Train connections to King's Cross and Euston from:

Hull, fastest travel time	2 hrs 45 mins
off-peak frequency	1 per hr
York, fastest travel time	2 hrs 13 mins
off-peak frequency	2 per hr

First commuter train to arrive in London at approximately 8.30 a.m.:

from Hull	5.23 a.m.
from York	6.55 a.m.

Approximate road distances to central London from:

Hull, (via M62, (M1))	215 miles
York (via A1M, (M1))	193 miles

Also close is Leeds airport with 6 international departures and scheduled flights to:
Heathrow, 2 to 8 per day
Gatwick, 1 to 3 per day

NORTHUMBERLAND, DURHAM AND

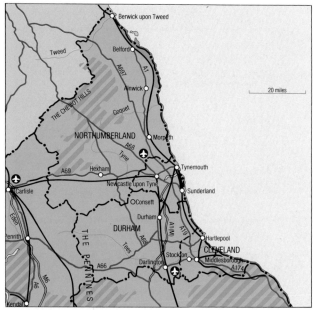

GEOGRAPHY

One of England's largest counties, Northumberland is roughly triangular in shape, its base being the river Tyne. It is also one of the least populated of the counties and contains wide areas of uninhabited countryside. In the south, Northumberland borders Durham. There is a high Pennine moorland in the west, lowering as one moves towards the east coast. To the west of the county, the upland Pennine landscape continues, with the Cheviot Hills dominating the scene. Further north, the Tweed forms the north-west boundary, with the broad acres of Kielder Forest covering much of the Border fells.

The Northumberland coastline is spectacular. It has a series of sandy beaches and dramatic rock cliffs, interspersed with castles and fishing villages. The beauty and character of the coast have been recognised by designation both as a Heritage Coast and as an Area of Outstanding Natural Beauty. Parallel to the coast is the coastal plain, a belt of farmland. A prominent feature of the Northumberland landscape is its castles. Among these, Bamburgh is probably the most visually rewarding coastal one, not only of the county, but probably of the whole country.

The south and south-east include large urban areas that are heavily industrialised, including the great coalfields. The climate of the county is cold, especially in the central and western highland belt. Rainfall tends to be light in the central and eastern areas, more heavy on the Cheviot Hills. The county contains five principal rivers. The Tyne flows from west to east and is heavily industrialised in its eastern lengths. The others are the Tweed, Aln, Coquet and Rede.

Northumberland was a frontier province for the Romans for almost 300 years, and contains much of Hadrian's Wall. After their departure, Northumberland became a 'cradle of Christianity', and an important centre was Holy Island.

Durham is, in many respects, an industrial county, with coal mining extensive in the north and south. However, it still retains wide expanses of unspoilt countryside. Moving across the county to the west, one encounters the Pennine hills, reaching 2,000 ft. and providing the source of the county's chief rivers, the Wear, Tees and Derwent. However, the actual birthplaces of the latter two lie outside Durham's boundaries. This moorland area is known as Weardale, and it boasts Britain's highest waterfall, High Force. The hills of the west give way to gentle, lowland farmland in the east, where forest and common are also to be found. The coastline of Durham varies from wide, sandy beaches at South Shields, to low-lying limestone cliffs.

The Romans built many forts and roads in the county, the purpose of these being to supply the legions manning Hadrian's Wall. Proximity to the Scottish Border resulted in continuous raids by the Scots. There were also numerous attacks from Europe, and castles such as Raby and Lumley are reminders of the coastal defences. Durham has its origins as a Palatinate of the Bishops of Durham, and also has a historic university.

The name Cleveland actually means 'land of cliffs', which gives some indication of some of the scenery. The coastline is a series of cliffs and beaches facing the North Sea. The central region is moorland, while the southern boundary with Yorkshire is an area of uplands known as the Cleveland Hills. The northern portion of the county tends to be of softer

CLEVELAND

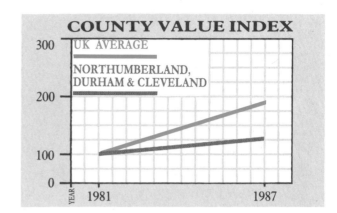

COUNTY VALUE INDEX

UK AVERAGE

NORTHUMBERLAND,
DURHAM & CLEVELAND

(Far left) **Bamburgh Castle, Northumberland** *(Kenneth Scowen). (Left)* **A fine Northumberland stone house considerably enlarged.**

scenery, with fertile farmland. The river Tees runs through the county, north-east to south-west.

MARKET TOWNS

The county town of Northumberland is Morpeth. Other towns are Alnwick, Hexham, Corbridge, Rothbury, Bellingham and Wooler.

Durham is, of course, its own county town, famous for its cathedral, ancient castle and university. Other market towns are Chester-le-Street, Barnard Castle and Bishop Auckland.

Middlesbrough is Cleveland's largest town, a sprawling industrial city, together with Stockton and Hartlepool. Other towns are Guisborough, Yarm, Loftus and Hart.

LEISURE

The three north-eastern counties between them include some celebrated hunts. Most renowned is the Percy, closely followed by the Morpeth, the Border, the Braes of Derwent, the Bewcastle, the Haydon, the Tynedale, the South Durham and the Cleveland (partly in Yorkshire). The whole region includes some of the finest open riding and walking country in the United Kingdom.

Fishing is controlled by the Northumbrian Water Authority, and includes not only the Tyne, Wear, Tees and their tributaries, but such celebrated rivers as the Coquet, with salmon, sea-trout and trout.

There are flat racing and racing under rules at Newcastle, with NH meetings at Hexham and Sedgefield.

Golf courses include Alnmouth, near Alnwick; Arcot Hall, Cramlington; Bamburgh Castle; Barnard Castle;

Berwick-upon-Tweed (designed by James Braid); Castle Eden and Peterlee (designed by Henry Cotton); Northumberland, Gosforth Park; and Seaton Carew.

GREAT HOUSES AND GARDENS

National Trust properties include Bellister Castle; Dunstanburgh Castle; Lindisfarne Castle on Holy Island, Berwick-upon-Tweed; large stretches of Hadrian's Wall; and the Farne Islands and much of the coastline.

Other houses and castles open to the public include Alnwick Castle, Bamburgh Castle, Warkworth Castle, Callaly Castle, Auckland Castle, Durham Castle, Raby Castle and Rokeby Park near Barnard Castle.

COMMUNICATIONS

Train connections to King's Cross and Euston from:
Carlisle, fastest travel time   3 hrs 55 mins
    off-peak frequency   1 per 2 hrs
Newcastle upon Tyne fastest travel time   3 hrs
    off-peak frequency   1 per hr

Approximate road distances to central London from:
Carlisle, (via M6, (M1))   307 miles
Newcasle, (via A1M, (M1))   274 miles

Airports: Carlisle has scheduled flights to:
    Heathrow Mon.-Fri. 2 per day.

Teesside: scheduled flights to:
    Heathrow, 3 to 6 per day
    Gatwick, 1 to 2 per day

Newcastle: scheduled flights to 19 international departures and:
    Heathrow, 3 to 6 per day
    Gatwick, 1 to 2 per day

LANCASHIRE AND CUMBRIA

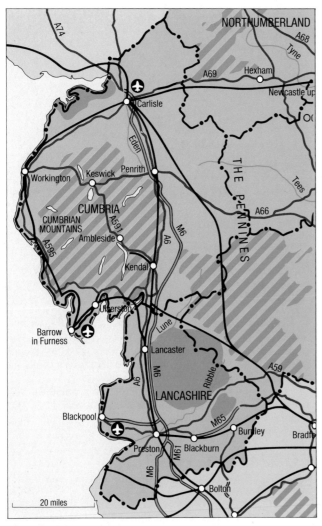

for its Lake District. This is located in the north-west and central area, and has been designated a National Park. It is an extremely popular tourist attraction, and becomes crowded during the summer months. The western boundary of the county is coastline, a picturesque length of countryside that includes the Sellafield nuclear plant. In the south-west is Barrow-in-Furness, an area that was involved in ship-building and has now moved on to the construction of submarines.

Although the Forestry Commission has been at work in many areas of Cumbria, expanses of open, deciduous woodland remain. Hugging river valleys, they provide a dark contrast to the smooth green fields, particularly in the south of the country. The climate is mild, with high levels of rainfall. A key point in Lancashire's history was the Wars of the Roses, when Lancashire was at war with Yorkshire. A great deal of present-day Lancashire is a legacy of the 19th century, and the rule of King cotton.

Cumbria has a history of repeated attacks and invasions from Scotland. There are, therefore, a large number of fortified houses and castles near the Border. The county once possessed a thriving mining industry and a woollen trade at

A typical stone cottage in Cumbria. *(Top right)* **Well-proportioned classical Lancashire house.** *(Below right)* **View over Haweswater in the Lake District** *(Tom Wright).*

GEOGRAPHY

The landscape of Lancashire ranges from coastline to Pennines, moorland to forest. The western border is a long stretch of bays and small cliffs; in the north reaching up towards the Lake District, and in the south embracing the holiday resorts of Blackpool and Morecambe. The south of the county is more populated than the north, with manufacturing and industrial centres.

In contrast to the southern landscape, the central area of Lancashire is moorland and undulating hill scenery. This upland area of the Trough of Bowland rises towards the east, and in the north adjoins the Pennine hill range. In the north east, a fairly extensive forested area leads up into Cumbria. The climate is mild, with high levels of rainfall. The main rivers are the Ribble and Lune.

Cumbria is a very beautiful county, perhaps most known

Kendal, but its main asset now is the Lake District, which has generated a profitable tourist industry.

MARKET TOWNS

Lancaster is the county town of Lancashire, and the only major town, together with the seaside resorts, north of Preston. Other towns are Bolton, Wigan, Clitheroe, Carnforth, Garstang, Colne and Ormskirk.

Carlisle is the county town of Cumbria. Other towns are Penrith, Kendal, Cockermouth, Barrow-in-Furness, Brampton, Alston, Keswick, Bowness, Appleby, Whitehaven, Workington and Kirby Stephen.

LEISURE

Foxhunting is with the Cumberland and Cumberland Farmers, with adjoining counties in the north of Cumbria; the Melbreak; the Eskdale and Ennerdale; the Blencathra, known as the John Peel foxhounds, with hounds that are said to trace their pedigree back to his time; the Ullswater; Lunesdale; and the Coniston.

The Grand National, the world's most celebrated steeplechase, is held at Aintree, north of Liverpool. There is also National Hunt racing at Cartmel. Both flat and National Hunt meetings are held at Haydock and Carlisle.

No area in Britain offers a wider range of different kinds of fishing, with salmon and trout rivers and lake fishing.

Golf is also very widely catered for. Among well-known courses are Royal Lytham St Annes, in Lancashire, and Silloth-on-Solway (originally Carlisle and Silloth) in Cumbria.

Sailing is offered both on the lakes of the Lake District and on the sea-coast. Lancashire has long been a leading cricket county, and the Old Trafford ground was bought by Manchester Cricket club as long ago as 1856.

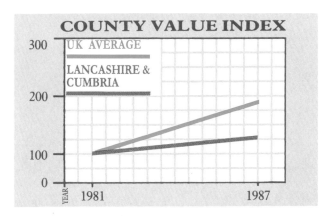

GREAT HOUSES AND GARDENS

National Trust properties in Lancashire include Gawthorpe Hall, near Burnley, and Rufford Old Hall, near Ormskirk. In Cumbria, National Trust properties range from Sizergh Castle, near Kendal, to Beatrix Potter's home, Hill Top, near Sawrey. Houses in private ownership, open to the public, include Hoghton Tower, near Preston; Meons Hall, near Southport; and Winole Hall, near St Helens, in Lancashire; and in Cumbria, Graythwaite Hall near Ulverston.

Agricultural shows include the Cumberland, held in the third week of July at Carlisle, and Westmorland County at Turriff at the beginning of August.

COMMUNICATIONS

 Train connections to King's Cross and Euston from:

Carlisle, fastest travel time	3 hrs 55 mins
off-peak frequency	1 per 2 hrs
Preston, fastest travel time	3 hrs
off-peak frequency	1 per hr

 Approximate road distances to central London from:

Carlisle (via M6, (M1))	307 miles
Preston (via M6, (M1))	218 miles

 Airports: Cumbria: Barrow in Furness has scheduled flights to:
Manchester Mon. to Fri. 3 per day
Carlisle has scheduled flights to:
Heathrow Mon. to Fri. 2 per day
Lancashire: Blackpool has scheduled flights to:
Dublin, 4 per week
Isle of Man, 1 to 3 per day
Belfast, 1 to 2 per day
Isle of Man has scheduled flights to:
Glasgow, 4 per week
Manchester, 2 to 3 per day
Liverpool, 2 to 4 per day
Heathrow, 1 to 4 per day

COUNTY VALUE INDEX

UK AVERAGE

LANCASHIRE & CUMBRIA

300
200
100
0
YEAR 1981   1987

SCOTLAND

SOUTH-WEST AND THE BORDERS

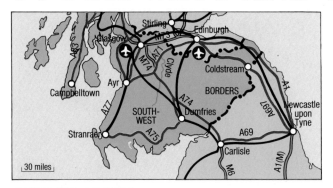

GEOGRAPHY

The south-west and the Border region of southern Scotland are two quite distinct areas: the east, generally wooded countryside, and the west, a miniature Highlands. The main hill ranges run south-west to north-east and are named Tweedsmuir, Moorfoot and Lammermuir. The main rivers are the Liddel, Teviot, Moffat, Yarrow and the Tweed, the latter forming the boundary between Scotland and England in its lower reaches. Not only do they provide excellent fishing, but they have been the base for a textile industry.

The south-east is lower-lying land, more intensively farmed. Its coastline is one of the sunniest places in Scotland from May to July. Rarely are there long spells of wet weather. In contrast, the south-west possesses all the features of a Highland landscape apart from its scale, comprising moorland, lochs and mountains. It is wetter than the east, and slightly warmer.

The Lowland Scot is of Anglo-Saxon origin. Numerous hill-forts and castles bear witness to the Border region of southern Scotland having been fought over since Roman times. During the Middle Ages, the Border shifted many times, until it was more or less settled on its present line in 1325. Union with England finally came in 1707. Traditionally this is Scotland's horse country. It also possesses numerous castles and fine country houses, mostly dating from the late 17th century onwards.

MARKET TOWNS

The principal town is Ayr. Other important towns include Kelso, Dumfries, Kudcudbright, Hawick, Selkirk, Peebles, Annan, Castle Douglas, Newton Stewart, Moffat, Coldstream, Jedburgh, Melrose, Duns, Galashiels, Girvan, Maybole, Stranraer, and Troon.

LEISURE

Only parts of southern Scotland are hunted. Packs include the Dumfriesshire, with kennels at Glenholm; the Liddesdale, with kennels near Hawick; the Jedforest, with kennels at Bonchester Bridge; the Duke of Buccleuch's, with kennels at St Boswells; the Lauderdale at Lauder; and the Berwickshire

at Duns. In Ayrshire are the Eglinton, with kennels at Earlston; and just north, the Lanarkshire and Renfrewshire, with kennels at Houston. There is flat and National Hunt racing at Ayr and N.H. meetings at Kelso.

There is a very wide choice of fishing waters. All fishing in Scotland is under the general jurisdiction of the Department of Agriculture and Fisheries for Scotland, Chester House, Gorgie Road, Edinburgh EH11 3AW, from whom can be obtained a list of District Fishing Boards. Waters range from the Annan in Dumfries and Galloway to the Tweed and its tributaries. The Clyde estuary rivals the

Ruined castle at Sanquhar, Dumfries and Galloway *(Peter Baker)*.

Solent as a yachting water, and offers some of the best sailing in Britain, in beautiful scenery.

Golf is, of course, a major attraction. Celebrated links along the Firth of Clyde include Prestwick, Ayr, Royal Troon, Turnberry and Western Gailes. Border courses range from Hawick eastward to Berwick-upon-Tweed.

GREAT HOUSES AND GARDENS

National Trust for Scotland properties include Culzean Castle and Country Park, on the coast south of Ayr; Threave Castle and Garden, near Castle Douglas; Brodick Castle and

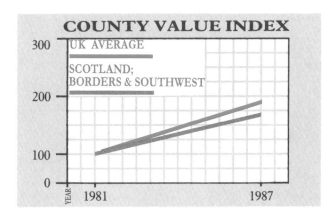

Country Park, and Goatfell, on the Isle of Arran; and considerable areas of open country, including the Grey Mare's Tail waterfall, near Loch St Mary, with 2,400 acres. On the Berwickshire coast the NTS has the St Abb's Head National Nature Reserve.

Other properties include Blairquhan Castle and Gardens, near Maybole; Bowhill, near Selkirk; Floors Castle, near Kelso; Manderston, near Duns; Mellerstain, near Gordon; Abbotsford House, Melrose, the home of Sir Walter Scott; and Thirlestane Castle, near Lauder.

Agricultural shows include Ayr, at the end of April; and the Border Union, at Kelso in late July.

(Left) **A splendid Galloway mansion with pedimented entranceway.**

COMMUNICATIONS

 Train connections to Euston from:

Stranraer, fastest travel time	9 hrs 25 mins
off-peak frequency	2 per day
Galashiels, fastest travel time	6 hrs
off-peak frequency	irregular
Dumfries, fastest travel time	5 hrs 3 mins
off-peak frequency	irregular

 Approximate road distances to central London from:

Stranraer (via A75, M6, M1)	515 miles
Galashiels (via A7, M6, M1)	346 miles
Dumfries (via A75, M6, M1)	312 miles

 Airports: Glasgow airport has scheduled flights to:
Heathrow, 6 to 12 per day
Gatwick, 4 per day

Edinburgh airport has scheduled flights to:
Heathrow, 6 to 10 per day
Gatwick, 3 per day

Bridge over the Nith at Dumfries *(Peter Baker).*

COUNTY VALUE INDEX

UK AVERAGE

SCOTLAND;
BORDERS & SOUTHWEST

300

200

100

0

YEAR   1981   1987

CENTRAL SCOTLAND

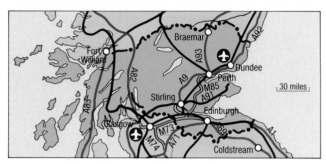

GEOGRAPHY

Central Scotland can be divided into two sections, the east and west. The eastern section contains Fife, Lothian and Tayside. The western area comprises Strathclyde. Generally the eastern area is lowland, although the land does begin to rise in the north. The southern area of this central part of Scotland has the country's capital, Edinburgh. Further north is an industrial belt, including the major cities of Stirling, Perth and Dundee.

The west is a mostly upland region, with mountains and deep sea lochs. Glasgow is the major city. The western coastline is broken up by a myriad of rocky or sandy bays and lochs. A sprinkling of historic castles lie along this sea border, interspersed with some of the finest gardens in the world. The climate is mild, and quite wet in the west, but dry in the east. The principal rivers are the Clyde, Forth and Tay. There are many large estates, castles and country houses in the region, the most famous of the castles being Edinburgh.

MARKET TOWNS

Glasgow is the major, industrial city, with the satellite towns of Paisley, Cumbernauld and Greenock. Perth, Stirling and Dundee are other major cities. Edinburgh is not only the capital of Scotland, but a world financial centre. Other important towns are Kilmarnock, East Kilbride, Hamilton, Lanark, Coatbridge, Livingston, Falkirk, Dunfermline, Creiff, Cupar, St Andrews, Arbroath and Forfar.

LEISURE

Most foxhunting is further south, but the region includes the Lanarkshire and Renfrewshire, with kennels at Houston; the Linlithgow and Stirlingshire with kennels at Linlithgow; and the Fife, with kennels at Ceres. There is, however, a wide range of shooting and stalking. Fishing, for salmon, sea-trout and trout, is widely available. See section 'Scotland, South-West and the Borders'.

There is flat racing at Hamilton, and flat and National Hunt racing at Edinburgh.

The region includes some of the world's most famous golf courses, notably St Andrews and Gleneagles. Gleneagles has a number of courses, including two designed by James Braid. St Andrews also has several courses, with green fees that are low by English standards. At St Andrews is the

clubhouse of the Royal and Ancient. In Fife are other historic courses, including Elie, the birthplace of James Braid.

GREAT HOUSES AND GARDENS

Properties of the National Trust for Scotland include, beside many in and around Edinburgh and Glasgow, the Palace at Culross; The House of The Binns, West Lothian; Falkland Palace and Garden, and Kellie Castle and Garden, Pittenweem. In the East Neuk of Fife are many small houses restored by the National Trust for Scotland and then sold

COUNTY VALUE INDEX

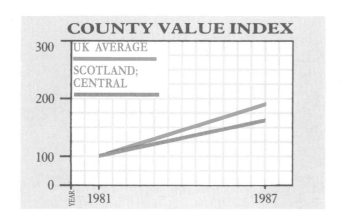

(Top) **Comfortable stone house among the heather of Central Scotland.** *(Below left)* **Converted tower house with stepped gables.** *(Below right)* **View across West Loch Tarbert on the Kintyre peninsula** *(Peter Baker).*

under covenant to ensure their future use and maintenance.

Other properties open to the public include Stirling Castle (in the care of the Secretary of State for Scotland), Earlshall Castle and Gardens, at Leuchars; Hill of Tarvit, a house not a hill, near Cupar; and Aberdour Castle, Fife.

AGRICULTURAL SHOWS

The Royal Highland Show, in spite of its name, is held not in the Highlands, but at Ingliston, Edinburgh, in the latter part of June.

COMMUNICATIONS

Train connections to Euston from:

Edinburgh, fastest travel time	4 hrs 55 mins
off-peak frequency	1 per hr
Glasgow, fastest travel time	5 hrs 15 mins
off-peak frequency	1 per 2 hrs
Stirling, fastest travel time	6 hrs
off-peak frequency	1 per day

Approximate road distances to central London from:

Edinburgh (via A68, A1(M))	378 miles
Glasgow (via A74, M6, M1)	397 miles
Stirling (via M80, M73, A74, M6, M1)	410 miles

Airports: Glasgow airport has scheduled flights to:
   Heathrow, 6 to 12 per day
   Gatwick, 4 per day

Edinburgh airport has scheduled flights to:
   Heathrow, 6 to 10 per day
   Gatwick, 3 per day

Dundee airport has scheduled flights to:
   Heathrow, 2 per week day

SCOTLAND: THE HIGHLANDS

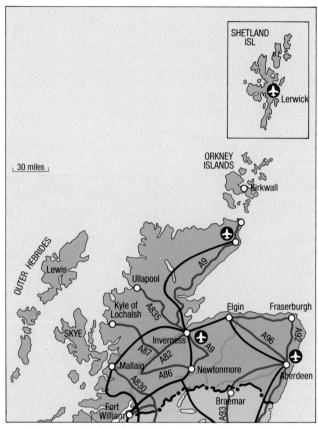

GEOGRAPHY

The Highlands of Scotland are separated from the Central Lowlands of Scotland by a line running from Stonehaven, south of Aberdeen on the north-east coast, to Helensburgh on the Firth of Clyde. In turn the Highlands themselves are divided by a narrow, deep depression running from the Moray Firth east to the Firth of Lorn. This line, a geological fault, runs through the Great Glen and contains Loch Ness, Loch Oich and Loch Lochy, and freshwater locks linked by the Caledonian Canal.

The principal mountain areas of the Highlands are of granite or other igneous rock. The resistant quality of these rocks has resulted in their forming the chief mountain complex of the British Isles. The Cairngorms to the east and Ben Nevis, in the west, together comprise the five British summits that reach a height of over 4,000 ft. The east tends to be less rugged.

Much of the landscape has been formed by glaciation — mountains and glens, combes and scree. There are also wide stretches of moorland. Once the area was far more wooded than it is now. However, remnants of natural oak communities exist, and more extensively, the native forests of Scots pine.

The coastline is spectacular, jutting out into the sea like 'the knuckles of a gigantic fist'. There are tall cliffs, pounded by winter storms, that give way to inlets and small bays where fishing communities nestle. Some have developed into larger ports, for example, Aberdeen and Lossiemouth, while others survive as tiny hamlets. Off Scotland's north-west coast are the Hebrides.

The larger of these islands, including Skye and Lewis, are inhabited, and regular ferry crossings connect them to the mainland and each other. Further north are the Orkney and Shetland islands, almost tree-less and exposed in the North Atlantic ocean. The climate can be harsh, with cold winters, moderated by the Atlantic but without hot summers.

Tourism is being fostered on an increasing scale, more so because the Highlands are poor in natural resources and have long been under the threat of depopulation. The development of winter sports has been particularly successful. Predominantly agricultural, much of the Highlands is used for sheep and cattle rearing. The most favourable agricultural project at present is forestry.

In the north and west of the Highlands are Highland Scots, of Gaelic origins. In the Orkneys and Shetlands the society is more akin to Scandinavia. The Northern Highlands were inhabited by Picts until the coming of the Norsemen in the 8th century.

MARKET TOWNS

The principal towns are Oban, Wick, Thurso, Inverness, Elgin, Fort William, Ullapool, Nairn, Tain, Invergordon, Dingwall, Kyle and Portree.

LEISURE

Though the Highlands has not been considered horse country, the region has nevertheless produced, and vigorously maintains, the native Highland pony, one of the biggest and strongest of our nine Mountain and Moorland breeds.

Fishing, shooting, particularly of driven grouse, and deer-stalking are not only Highland sports but a very valuable part of the Highland economy, drawing in money at one time mainly from England, now increasingly from other industrialised countries.

Highland Games, held annually at Braemar and other centres, maintain traditional Highland athletic sports and increasingly attract tourism. There is excellent sailing off the west coast, and in the waters between the Hebrides and the mainland, but it is not for the unskilled. There is golf in most centres, many of the courses being in magnificent Highland settings, notably that at Kingussie.

There is an infinite range of hill-walking and climbing, but in general the Highlands must be treated with respect.

(Top right) **Harled walls and tiled roofs: a typical Highland house.** *(Below right)* **Eilean Donan Castle on Loch Duich** *(Peter Baker).*

GREAT HOUSES AND GARDENS

The National Trust for Scotland has widespread properties in the Highlands, though many are designed to protect mountain scenery and wildlife, such as the vast 16,000-acre estate of Torridon, in Ross and Cromarty. Among the peaks are Beinn Eighe (3,309 ft.) and Liathach (3,456 ft.).

Among celebrated gardens are Inverewe, near Pool Ewe, in the west coast, a sub-tropical garden made possible in this northerly latitude by the warm currents of the North Atlantic Drift. The Trust also owns the island of Iona, of great Christian significance because it was here that St Columba arrived from Ireland in AD 563, bringing the Gospel to Scotland. The Trust's houses and gardens include Fyvie Castle, Grampian; Haddo House, Gordon; Pitmedden Garden, north of Aberdeen; Crathes Castle and Garden, west of Aberdeen; and Craigievar Castle, Gordon.

Other properties open to the public include Dunrobin Castle, Golspie, home of the Earls and Dukes of Sutherland for 800 years; and Blair Castle, Pitlochry, home of the 10th Duke of Atholl, where he still maintains a private army.

AGRICULTURAL SHOWS

Scotland's principal show, the Royal Highland, is held, in spite of its name, at Ingliston, Edinburgh, in the latter part of June.

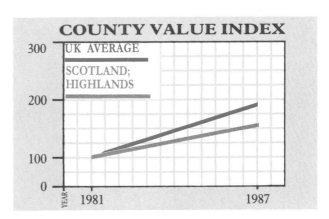

COUNTY VALUE INDEX

UK AVERAGE

SCOTLAND; HIGHLANDS

300
200
100
0

YEAR 1981   1987

COMMUNICATIONS

Train connections to Euston from:
Inverness, fastest travel time   8 hrs 42 mins
        off-peak frequency   5 per day (Mon. to Sat.)
Thurso, fastest travel time   13 hrs 7 mins
        off-peak frequency   5 per day (Mon. to Sat.)
Fort William, fastest travel time   12 hrs 50 mins
        off-peak frequency
                    1-2 per day (Mon. to Sat.)

Approximate road distances to central London from:
Inverness (via A9, M80, M73, M74, A74, M6, M4)   536 miles
Thurso (via A859, A9, M90, M8, M74, M6, M1)
                    645 miles
Fort William (via A82, M74, M6, M1)   497 miles

Airports: Inverness airport has scheduled flights to:
    Heathrow, 2 to 3 per day

Aberdeen has scheduled flights to:
    Heathrow, 2 to 4 per day.
    Gatwick, 2 per day

Wick airport has scheduled flights to:
    Aberdeen, 1 to 2 per day (not Sun.)
    Edinburgh, 1 to 2 per day (not Sun.)
    Inverness, 2 per week day
    Kirkwall, 2 to 3 per day (not Sun.)

Kirkwall airport has scheduled flights to:
    Aberdeen, 2 per day (not Sun.)
    Birmingham, 1 per day (not Sun.)
    Inverness, 1 to 3 per day (not Sun.)
    Lerwick, 1 to 2 per day (not Sun.)

Lerwick airport has flights to the Shetlands and the Orkneys

VALUE AT A GLANCE

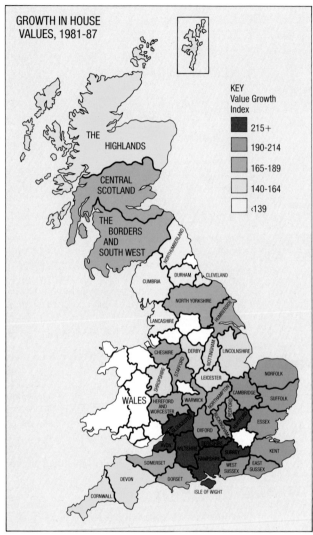

GROWTH IN HOUSE VALUES, 1981-87

KEY
Value Growth Index

- 215+
- 190-214
- 165-189
- 140-164
- ‹139

THE HIGHLANDS

CENTRAL SCOTLAND

THE BORDERS AND SOUTH WEST

NORTHUMBERLAND

CUMBRIA

DURHAM

CLEVELAND

NORTH YORKSHIRE

LANCASHIRE

HUMBERSIDE

CHESHIRE

DERBY

NOTTINGHAM

LINCOLNSHIRE

SHROPSHIRE

STAFFORD

LEICESTER

NORFOLK

WALES

HEREFORD AND WORCESTER

WARWICK

NORTHAMPTON

CAMBRIDGE

SUFFOLK

BUCKINGHAM

BEDFORD

HERTFORD

ESSEX

GLOUCESTER

OXFORD

AVON

WILTSHIRE

BERKSHIRE

SURREY

KENT

SOMERSET

HAMPSHIRE

WEST SUSSEX

EAST SUSSEX

DEVON

DORSET

CORNWALL

ISLE OF WIGHT

Growth in House Values, 1981-87.

A frequent topic of conversation in recent years has been the growth in the value of the country house. Not surprisingly, all agree that the greatest growth during the last five years has taken place closest to London where the demand for houses has been fuelled by the general level of affluence. At the same time, vastly improved communications have encouraged growth in some areas where it would have been hardly imaginable a few years ago. By contrast, the Northern Counties have shown only a modest growth, being as yet little affected by commuter pressures. In addition to actual growth, the Capital Gains Tax concession to main residence continues to underpin the attraction of investment in a country house.

Significant variations in the size of the price movement exist within the country, with distance from London being the most important influence. Predictably, the largest price increases have been in the Home Counties, notably Berkshire, Hampshire, Hertfordshire and Surrey, which are the traditional, commuter-favoured counties. The band of high-value appreciation extends westwards from London as far as Wiltshire and Gloucestershire. The latter's emergence in 1987 with a value rise comparable to those of the Home Counties is almost entirely due to the increasingly easy access to the capital by road and rail.

Following closely behind in terms of price rises since 1981 is the eastern group of counties around London, ranging from Sussex through Kent to East Anglia. Although not showing the 2½-fold increase of their western counterparts, house values here have more than doubled over the 5-year period. Most of this upsurge can be attributed to improved communications, particularly the M25 completion in Kent, the M11 extension in Cambridgeshire and the A12 improvements in Essex and Suffolk.

The influence which the capital exerts upon adjoining counties, such as Kent and Surrey, has resulted in their displaying two distinct price regions, based upon proximity to London. In some counties this pattern is becoming less pronounced, as the daily reach of the commuter is extended. The county value graphs disguise the actual spread of figures, as the average evens out the discrepancies.

The theme of a link between improved communications and value growth applies to many of the counties. The pattern of improvements to motorways, main roads and 125 Intercity lines is a major factor in the shaping of regional house prices. The marked rise in house prices in Hampshire is due to the efficient travelling facilities of both the railways and the M4, A303 and M3 corridors. The price rise is expected to accelerate in Wiltshire, Somerset and Dorset as the road system is improved in those counties. South Oxfordshire has enjoyed efficient links with London in recent years, as is reflected in the growth in the value of the area's country houses. The beneficial influence of better roads will be extended to the north of the county with the new link between London and Birmingham. Similarly it will shortly become more attractive to live in and commute from Warwickshire, whether working in London or Birmingham. Northamptonshire and Bedfordshire have traditionally been less popular areas for London commuters, but the modest price increases which they have experienced between 1981 and 1987 are still well in excess of 1½ times.

The City of Birmingham has had an equally important influence upon some of the counties which border it. Warwickshire, Hereford and Worcester have become increasingly popular areas for a country house which is within easy commuting distance. In the north-west, Manchester has exerted a similar influence upon Cheshire and to a lesser extent on Staffordshire and north-west Derbyshire.

It is well known that property prices in the northern half of the country have not risen as fast as elsewhere. The exception is Yorkshire, where the increases are equal to the

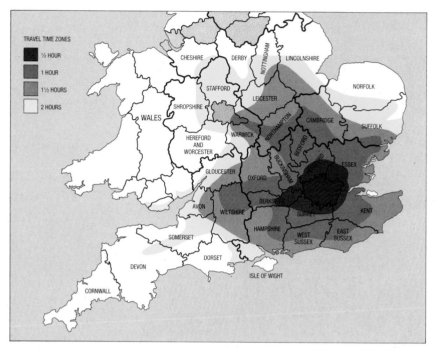

Fastest travel times from London.

TRAVEL TIME ZONES
- ½ HOUR
- 1 HOUR
- 1½ HOURS
- 2 HOURS

best increases near Birmingham and Manchester. Some buyers showing interest in the area have accepted the idea of long-distance commuting, as increasing emphasis is placed upon the amenities of living in the country. This attitude is reflected in a growing tendency towards weekend commuting, thus enabling the country house to be in an area further afield than the traditional southern counties. Certainly in Yorkshire prices are rising as increasing demand for good country houses leaves the market in short supply. By contrast, counties in the East Midlands have seen lesser increases which are more akin to those in Shropshire than the south-east.

The English counties north of Yorkshire have achieved the lowest price appreciation of all. This is not a result of inferior properties, but is due entirely to a lack of demand. Much of Northumberland is of exceptional beauty, but it lies in an awkward position for the commuter, too distant from either Edinburgh or Newcastle. The generally depressed nature of the local economy has kept demand low.

Scotland has experienced substantial price rises over the five years of this survey, particularly in the Borders, the south-west and central Scotland. Not only do these regions possess good road and rail connections to the commercial centres of Glasgow and Edinburgh, but they also provide efficient means of travel to and from London. The Highlands have not been left behind in terms of the country house market, showing a modest but respectable rise in values over the years 1981 to 1987. The price rises reflect the continuing

demand for a home in perhaps the most dramatic countryside of all.

The vexed question of value for money between the counties is not easily solved. In the days before the improvements in communications, the railways had set a very definite limit to commuter travelling. Those limits are being continually pushed further away from the great conurbations, so that it can now be said that when someone sees a house they really want, it does not matter nearly so much in which part of the country it is. Given that some counties have always been more popular than others, it is to be expected that places of high prices for country houses will continue to be supported by the keen interest of active buyers.

What is far more difficult to determine in general terms is how much of a house should be considered strictly as an investment. In a sense, the answer is only that part above and beyond the immediate living and entertaining requirement. Only this is true speculative investment, as we all have to live somewhere. In the same sense, there could be little meaningful comparison between that immediate need and any alternative sort of investment. Direct comparisons can only be made with house values in other places. However, the 'excess' paid for extras in the form of amenity and location could perhaps bear direct comparison with such accepted measures as the *Financial Times* All Share Index, which has risen well over three times in the period examined in this *Guide*. Although in average growth terms even the most successful county has not achieved such an increase, it is well known that the principal private residence does not suffer Capital Gains Tax on growth in value. The country house as the main residence is thus in a privileged tax position. After allowing for tax where payable, the net gain in the best growth areas exceeds that shown for the Index, whilst many other counties are almost equally well placed. Many will have already made the calculation that buying a country house becomes ever more attractive when it allows the unique enjoyment of a well-placed investment in addition. Unlike other investments, if the economy moves to suppress investment growth, the country house can still be enjoyed for its intrinsic worth.

The composite graph shows those Home Counties which have seen most growth in the past five years. What is impossible to determine with certainty is where greatest growth will show in the next few years. Houses in those counties near to London certainly maintain their value, but equal growth could also come where road communications

One of a Set of Six 18th c. Portuguese Dining Chairs 43" H 21" W 16" D.

Baggott Church Street Limited

ANTIQUE DEALERS

Church Street, Stow-on-the-Wold,
Gloucestershire GL541BB
Telephone: Stow-on-the-Wold (0451) 30370

Fine furniture for the
English Country House

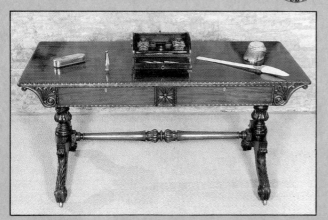

Late Regency Mahogany Writing Table 57" W.

Georgian Mahogany Dumbwaiter 41" H.

George III Mahogany Secretaire Bookcase 62" W.

Pair Sheraton Mahogany Tea Tables 36" W.

with the capital are improved next. So attention may be directed to Somerset and Dorset with the extension of the A303 dual carriageways, to Warwickshire and north Oxfordshire with the M40 link, to Suffolk with the A12 improvements and south-east Kent with the M20. The recent revolution in working habits for many in the City has meant that the zone of country houses nearest to London has become even more attractive, although it already carries a premium, because it has the best communications.

Many consider interest rates and the availability of funding to be the most crucial supports to house values and demand, yet disposable income to pay for the funding and the almost complete absence of equivalent properties to rent must be equally important factors. Planning restrictions mean there are relatively few opportunities to build in the style required, so the supply of country houses remains virtually static. Meanwhile the demands of the buyers are maintained by increasing affluence and improved communications. Those studying such matters maintain that, in the long term, even allowing for inflation, there has been a steady and continuous climb in real house prices. Despite the booms and depressions of the last two decades, the tendency remains clearly upwards, with current average prices near the long-term trend. Thus the scope for further increases remains.

In all the talk of the growth in values in different parts of the country, there still remains a vast discrepancy in price between any country house near to London and its equivalent in terms of accommodation and amenities further away. Though working very much in favour of anyone moving house to a cheaper county, the discrepancy tells heavily against those who have to consider moving to the south-east. Another factor not to be overlooked when considering growth in value is the relationship between the equity and the borrowed money, if the latter is used for purchase. The borrowed money does not normally attract any capital growth, which therefore accrues entirely to the equity portion. In a typical purchase of a country house, 50 per cent, perhaps, of the purchase price may be equity. A doubling in value of the house in five years means a four-fold growth in the value of the owner's equity. Other alternative investments rarely offer, if at all, such superb opportunities for growth of one's own equity at the expense of the borrowings.

In summary, the last five years have seen spectacular growth in the southern counties near London, while other conurbations have had their own local influences. Over the country as a whole, demand and prices have held up, because of the continued attraction of living in Britain's countryside, even whilst working in a city. All the present indications are that these influences will continue to uphold the value of investment in a country house.

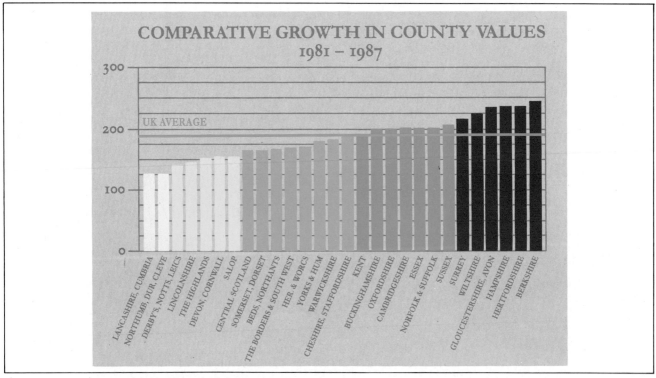

Comparative Growth in County Values, 1981-1987.

For a little place like this...

A TOWN HOUSE IN LONDON

**...OR
A MANSION IN THE COUNTRY**

**...OR
A FARMHOUSE IN TUSCANY**

...read
COUNTRY LIFE
for the pick of the finest houses every Thursday

THE KNIGHT FRANK & RUTLEY GROUP

Knight Frank and Rutley is one of the largest international real estate firms in the world operating through 43 different offices in Western Europe, west and central Southern Africa, North America, the Far East and Australia.

The firm has experience in over 60 different countries, and their clients include governments, international agencies, banks, corporations, institutions, companies and private individuals.

For over 90 years the name of Knight Frank and Rutley has been synonymous with the sale of some of the finest houses and estates throughout the British Isles.

Head Office:
20 Hanover Square, London W1R 0AH
Telephone: 01-629 8171, Telex: 265384
Fax: 01-493 4114

UK Offices:
City of London ● Cirencester ● Hungerford
Docklands ● Edinburgh ● Leeds
Knightsbridge ● Glasgow ● Sherborne
Ascot ● Guildford ● Shrewsbury
Chipping Norton ● Hereford
Stratford-upon-Avon

International Offices:
Australia ● Belgium ● Botswana ● France
Hong Kong ● Malaysia ● Nigeria ● Singapore
United States of America ● Zimbabwe